tredition®

tredition was established in 2006 by Sandra Latusseck and Soenke Schulz. Based in Hamburg, Germany, tredition offers publishing solutions to authors and publishing houses, combined with world-wide distribution of printed and digital book content. tredition is uniquely positioned to enable authors and publishing houses to create books on their own terms and without conventional manu-facturing risks.

For more information please visit: www.tredition.com

TREDITION CLASSICS

This book is part of the TREDITION CLASSICS series. The creators of this series are united by passion for literature and driven by the intention of making all public domain books available in printed format again - worldwide. Most TREDITION CLASSICS titles have been out of print and off the bookstore shelves for decades. At tredition we believe that a great book never goes out of style and that its value is eternal. Several mostly non-profit literature projects provide content to tredition. To support their good work, tredition donates a portion of the proceeds from each sold copy. As a reader of a TREDITION CLASSICS book, you support our mission to save many of the amazing works of world literature from oblivion. See all available books at www.tredition.com.

Project Gutenberg

The content for this book has been graciously provided by Project Gutenberg. Project Gutenberg is a non-profit organization founded by Michael Hart in 1971 at the University of Illinois. The mission of Project Gutenberg is simple: To encourage the creation and distribu-tion of eBooks. Project Gutenberg is the first and largest collection of public domain eBooks.

Roving East and Roving West

Edward Verrall Lucas

Imprint

This book is part of TREDITION CLASSICS

Author: Edward Verrall Lucas
Cover design: Buchgut, Berlin – Germany

Publisher: tredition GmbH, Hamburg - Germany
ISBN: 978-3-8424-2953-6

www.tredition.com
www.tredition.de

ROVING EAST

AND

ROVING WEST

BY

E. V. LUCAS

TO

E. L. L.

MY HOST AT RAISINA

"Yes, Sir, there are two objects of curiosity, e.g., the Christian world and the Mahometan world." — DR. JOHNSON.

"Motion recollected in tranquillity." — WORDSWORTH (*very nearly*).

INDIA

NOISELESS FEET

Although India is a land of walkers, there is no sound of footfalls. Most of the feet are bare and all are silent: dark strangers overtake one like ghosts.

Both in the cities and the country some one is always walking. There are carts and motorcars, and on the roads about Delhi a curious service of camel omnibuses, but most of the people walk, and they walk ever. In the bazaars they walk in their thousands; on the long, dusty roads, miles from anywhere, there are always a few, approaching or receding.

It is odd that the only occasion on which Indians break from their walk into a run or a trot is when they are bearers at a funeral, or have an unusually heavy head-load, or carry a piano. Why there is so much piano- carrying in Calcutta I cannot say, but the streets (as I feel now) have no commoner spectacle than six or eight merry, half-naked fellows, trotting along, laughing and jesting under their burden, all with an odd, swinging movement of the arms.

One of one's earliest impressions of the Indians is that their hands are inadequate. They suggest no power.

Not only is there always some one walking, but there is always some one resting. They repose at full length wherever the need for sleep takes them; or they sit with pointed knees. Coming from England one is struck by so much inertness; for though the English labourer can be lazy enough he usually rests on his feet, leaning against walls: if he is a land labourer, leaning with his back to the support; if he follows the sea, leaning on his stomach.

It was interesting to pass on from India and its prostrate philosophers with their infinite capacity for taking naps, to Japan, where there seems to be neither time nor space for idlers. Whereas in India one has continually to turn aside in order not to step upon a sleeping figure— the footpath being a favourite dormitory—in Japan no one is ever doing nothing, and no one appears to be weary or poor.

India, save for a few native politicians and agitators, strikes one as a land destitute of ambition. In the cities there are infrequent signs of progress; in the country none. The peasants support life on as little as they can, they rest as much as possible and their carts and implements are prehistoric. They may believe in their gods, but fatalism is their true religion. How little they can be affected by civilisation I learned from a tiny settlement of bush-dwellers not twenty miles from Bombay, close to that beautiful lake which has been transformed into a reservoir, where bows and arrows are still the only weapons and rats are a staple food. And in an hour's time, in a car, one could be telephoning one's friends or watching a cinema!

THE SAHIB

I did not have to wait to reach India for that great and exciting moment when one is first called "Sahib." I was addressed as "Sahib," to my mingled pride and confusion, at Marseilles, by an attendant on the steamer which I joined there. Later I grew accustomed to it, although never, I hope, blasé; but to the end my bearer fascinated me by alluding to me as Master—not directly, but obliquely: impersonally, as though it were some other person that I knew, who was always with me, an *alter ego* who could not answer for himself: "Would Master like this or that?" "At what time did Master wish to be called?"

And then the beautiful "Salaam"!

I was sorry for the English doomed to become so used to Eastern deference that they cease to be thrilled.

THE PASSING SHOW

It is difficult for a stranger to India, especially when paying only a brief visit, to lose the impression that he is at an exhibition—in a section of a World's Fair. How long it takes for this delusion to wear off I cannot say. All I can say is that seven weeks are not enough. And never does one feel it more than in the bazaar, where movement is incessant and humanity is so packed and costumes are so diverse, and where the suggestion of the exhibition is of course heightened by the merchants and the stalls. What one misses is any vantage point—anything resembling a chair at the Café de la Paix in Paris, for instance—where one may sit at ease and watch the wonderful changing spectacle going past. There are in Indian cities no such places. To observe the life of the bazaar closely and be unobserved is almost impossible.

It would be extraordinarily interesting to sit there, beside some well- informed Anglo-Indian or Indo-Anglian, and learn all the minutiæ of caste and be told who and what everybody was: what the different ochre marks signified on the Hindu foreheads; what this man did for a living, and that; and so forth. Even without such an informant I was never tired of drifting about the native quarters in whatever city I found myself and watching the curiously leisurely and detached commercial methods of the dealers—the money lenders reclining on their couches; the pearl merchants with their palms full of the little desirable jewels; the silversmiths hammering; the tailors cross-legged; the whole Arabian Nights pageant. All the shops seem to be overstaffed, unless an element of detached inquisitiveness is essential to business in the East. No transaction is complete without a few watchful spectators, usually youths, who apparently are employed by the establishment for the sole purpose of exhibiting curiosity.

I picked up a few odds and ends of information, by degrees, but only the more obvious: such as that the slight shaving of the Mohammedan's upper lip is to remove any impediment to the utterance of the name of Allah; that the red-dyed beards are a record that their wearers have made the pilgrimage to Mecca; that the respirator often worn by the Jains is to prevent the death of even a fly in inhalation. I was shown a Jain woman carefully emptying a piece of wood with holes in it into the road, each hole containing a louse which had crawled there during the night but must not be killed. The Jains adore every living creature; the Hindus chiefly the cow. As for this divinity, she drifts about the cities as though they were built for her, and one sees the passers-by touching her, hoping for sanctity or a blessing. A certain sex inequality is, however, only too noticeable, and particularly in and about Bombay, where the bullock cart is so common—the bullock receiving little but blows and execration from his drivers.

The sacred pigeon is also happy in Bombay, being fed copiously all day long; and I visited there a Hindu sanctuary, called the Pingheripole, for every kind of animal—a Home of Rest or Asylum—where even pariah dogs are fed and protected.

I was told early of certain things one must not do: such as saluting with the left hand, which is the dishonourable one of the pair, and refraining carefully, when in a temple or mosque, from touching anything at all, because for an unbeliever to touch is to desecrate. I was told also that a Mohammedan grave always gives one the points of the compass, because the body is buried north and south with the head at the north, turned towards Mecca. The Hindus have no graves.

In India the Occidental, especially if coming from France as I did, is struck by the absence of any out-of-door communion between men and women. In the street men are with men, women with women. Most women lower their eyes as a man approaches, although when the woman is a Mohammedan and young one is often conscious of a bright black glance through the veil. There is no public fondling, nothing like the familiar demonstrations of affection that we are accustomed to in Paris and London (more so during the War and since) and in New York. Nothing so offends and surprises the Indian as this want of restraint and shame on our part, and in Japan I learned that the Japanese share the Indian view.

It seemed to me that the chewing of the betel-nut is more prevalent in Bombay than elsewhere. One sees it all over India; everywhere are moving jaws with red juice trickling; but in Bombay there are more vendors of the rolled-up leaves and more crimson splashes on pavement and wall. It is an unpleasant habit, but there is no doubt that teeth are ultimately the whiter for it. Even though I was instructed in the art of betel-nut chewing by an Indian gentleman of world-wide fame in the cricket field, from whom I would willingly learn anything, I could not endure the experience.

Most nations, I suppose, look upon the dances of other nations with a certain perplexity. Such glimpses, for example, as I had in America of the movement known as the Shimmie Shake filled me with alarm, while Orientals have been known to display boredom at the Russian Ballet. Personally I adore the Russian Ballet, but I found the Nautch very fatiguing. It is at once too long and too monotonous, but I dare say that if one could follow the words of the accompanying songs, or cantillations, the result might be more entertaining. That would not, however, improve the actual dancing, in which I was disappointed. In Japan, on the other hand, I succumbed completely to the odd, hypnotic mechanism of the Geisha, the accompaniments to which are more varied, or more acceptable to my ear, than the Indian music. But I shall always remember the sounds of the distant, approaching or receding, snake- charmers' piping, heard through the heat, as it so often is on Sundays in Calcutta. To my inward ear that is India's typical melody; and it has relationship to the Punch and Judy allurement of our childhood.

It was in Bombay that I saw my first fakir, and in Harrison Road, Calcutta, my last. There had been so long a series in between that I was able to confirm my first impression. I can now, therefore, generalise safely when saying that all these strange creatures resemble a blend of Tolstoi and Mr. Bernard Shaw. Imagine such a hybrid, naked save for a loin cloth, and smeared all over with dust, and you have a holy man in the East. The Harrison Road fakir, who passed on his way along the crowded pavement unconcerned and practically unobserved, was white with ashes and was beating a piece of iron as a wayward child might be doing. He was followed by a boy, but no effort was made to collect alms. It is true philosophy to be prepared to live in such a state of simplicity. Most of the problems of life would dissolve and vanish if one could reduce one's needs to the frugality of a fakir. I have thought often of him since I returned, in London, to all the arrears of work and duty and the liabilities that accumulate during a long holiday; but never more so than when confronted by a Peace-time tailor's bill.

INDIA'S BIRDS

One of the first peculiarities of Bombay that I noticed and never lost sight of was the kites. The city by day is never without these spies, these sentries. From dawn to dusk the great unresting birds are sailing over it, silent and vigilant. Whenever you look up, there they are, criss-crossing in the sky, swooping and swerving and watching. After a while one begins to be nervous: it is disquieting to be so continually under inspection. Now and then they quarrel and even fight: now and then one will descend with a rush and rise carrying a rat or other delicacy in its claws; but these interruptions of the pattern are only momentary. For the rest of the time they swirl and circle and never cease to watch. Bombay also has its predatory crows, who are so bold that it is unsafe to leave any bright article on the veranda table. Spectacles, for example, set up a longing in their hearts which they make no effort to control. But these birds are everywhere. At a wayside station just outside Calcutta, in the early morning, the passengers all had tea, and when it was finished and the trays were laid on the platform, I watched the crows, who were perfectly aware of this custom and had been approaching nearer and nearer as we drank, dart swiftly to the sugar basins and carry off the lumps that remained. The crow, however, is, comparatively speaking, a human being; the kite is something alien and a cause of fear, and the traveller in India never loses him. His eye is as coldly attentive to Calcutta as to Bombay.

It is, of course, the indigenous birds of a country that emphasise its foreignness far more than its people. People can travel. Turbaned heads are, for example, not unknown in England; but to have green parrots with long tails flitting among the trees, as they used to flit in my host's garden in Bombay, is to be in India beyond question. At Raisina we had mynahs and the babblers, or "Seven Sisters," in great profusion, and also the King Crow with his imposing tail; while the little striped squirrels were everywhere. These merry restless little rodents do more than run and scamper and leap: they seem to be positively lifted into space by their tails. Their stripes (as every one knows) came directly from the hand of God, recording for ever how, on the day of creation, He stroked them by way of approval.

No Indian bird gave me so much pleasure to watch as the speckled kingfishers, which I saw at their best on the Jumna at Okhla. They poise in the air above the water with their long bills pointed downwards at a right-angle to their fluttering bodies, searching the depths for their prey; and then they drop with the quickness of thought into the stream. The other kingfisher — coloured like ours but bigger — who waits on an overhanging branch, I saw too, but the evolutions of the hovering variety were more absorbing.

When one is travelling by road, the birds that most attract the notice are the peacocks and the giant cranes; while wherever there are cattle in any numbers there are the white paddy birds, feeding on their backs — the birds from which the osprey plumes are obtained. One sees, too, many kinds of eagle and hawk. In fact, the ornithologist can never be dull in this country.

Wild animals I had few opportunities to observe, although a mongoose at Raisina gave me a very amusing ten minutes. At Raisina, also, the jackals came close to the house at night; and on an early morning ride in a motorcar to Agra we passed a wolf, and a little later were most impudently raced and outdistanced by a blackbuck, who, instead of bolting into security at the sight or sound of man, ran, or rather, advanced — for his progress is mysterious and magical — beside us for some forty yards and then, — with a laugh, put on extra speed (we were doing perhaps thirty miles an hour) and disappeared ahead. All about Muttra we dispersed monkeys up the trees and into the bushes as we approached. Next to the parrots it is the monkeys that most convince the traveller that he is in a strange tropical land. And the flying foxes. Nothing is more strange than a tree full of these creatures sleeping pendant by day, or their silent swift black movements by night.

I saw no snakes wild, but in the Bacteriological Laboratory at Parel in Bombay, which Lt.-Col. Glen Liston controls with so much zeal and resourcefulness, I was shown the process by which the antidotes to snake poisoning are prepared, for dispersion through the country. A cobra or black snake is released from his cage and fixed by the attendant with a stick pressed on his neck a little below the head. The snake is then firmly and safely held just above this point between the finger and thumb, and a tumbler, with a piece of flannel round its edge, is proffered to it to bite. As the snake bites, a clear yellow fluid, like strained honey in colour and thickness, flows into the glass from the poison fangs. This poison is later injected in small doses into the veins of horses kept carefully for the purpose, and then, in due course, the blood of the horses is tapped in order to make the anti-toxin. Wonderful are the ways of science! The Laboratory is also the headquarters of the Government's constant campaign against malaria and guinea worm, typhoid and cholera, and, in a smaller degree, hydrophobia. But nothing, I should guess, would ever get sanitary sense into India, except in almost negligible patches.

THE TOWERS OF SILENCE

The Parsees have made Bombay their own, more surely even than the Scotch possess Calcutta. Numerically very weak, they are long-headed and far- sighted beyond any Indian and are better qualified to traffick and to control. All the cotton mills are theirs, and theirs the finest houses in the most beautiful sites. When that conflict begins between the Hindus and the Mohammedans which will render India a waste and a shambles, it is the Parsees who will occupy the high places—until a more powerful conqueror arrives.

Bombay has no more curious sight than the Towers of Silence, the Parsee cemetery; and one of the first questions that one is asked is if one has visited them. But when the time came for me to ascend those sinister steps on Malabar Hill I need hardly say that my companion was a many years' resident of Bombay who, although he had long intended to go there, had hitherto neglected his opportunities. Throughout my travels I was, it is pleasant to think, in this way the cause of more sightseeing in others than they might ever have suffered. To give but one other instance typical of many—I saw Faneuil Hall in Boston in the company of a Bostonian some thirty years of age, whose office was within a few yards of this historic and very interesting building, and whose business is more intimately associated with culture than any other, but who had never before crossed the threshold.

The Towers of Silence, which are situated in a very beautiful park, with little temples among the trees and flowers, consist of five circular buildings, a model of one of which is displayed to visitors. Inside the tower is an iron grating on which the naked corpses are laid, and no sooner are they there than the awaiting vultures descend and consume the flesh. I saw these grisly birds sitting expectantly in rows on the coping of the towers, and the sight was almost too gruesome. Such is their voracity that the body is a skeleton in an hour or so. The Parsees choose this method of dissolution because since they worship fire they must not ask it to demean itself with the dead; and both earth and water they hold also too sacred to use for burial. Hence this strange and—at the first blush—repellant compromise. The sight of the cemetery that awaits us in England is rarely cheering, but if to that cemetery were attached a regiment of cruel and hideous birds of prey we should shudder indeed. Whether the Parsees shudder I cannot say, but they give no sign of it. They build their palaces in full view of these terrible Towers, pass, on their way to dinner parties, luxuriously in Rolls-Royces beside the trees where the vultures roost, and generally behave themselves as if this were the best possible of worlds and the only one. And I think they are wise.

Oriental apathy, or, at any rate, unruffled receptiveness, may carry its owner very far, and yet if these vultures cause no misgivings, no chills at the heart, I shall be surprised. As for those olive-skinned Parsee girls, with the long oval faces and the lustrous eyes—how must it strike them?

It was not till I went to the caves of Elephanta that I saw vultures in their marvellous flight. It is here that they breed, and the sky was full of them at an incredible distance up, resting on their great wings against the wind, circling and deploying. At this height they are magnificent. But seen at close quarters they are horrible, revolting. On a day's hunting which I shall describe later I was in at the death of a gond, or swamp-deer, at about noon, and we returned for the carcase about three hours later, only to find it surrounded by some hundreds of these birds tearing at it in a kind of frenzy of gluttony. They were not in the least disconcerted by our approach, and not until the bearers had taken sticks to them would they leave. The heavy half-gorged flapping of a vulture's wings as it settles itself to a new aspect of its repast is the most disgusting sight I have seen.

To revert to the Towers of Silence, one is brought very near to death everywhere in the East. We have our funeral corteges at home, with sufficient frequency, but they do not emphasize the thought of the necessary end of all things as do the swathed corpses that one meets so often being carried through the streets, on their way to this or that burning place. In Bombay I met several every day, with their bearers and followers all in white, and all moving with the curious trot that seems to be reserved for such obsequies. There were always, also, during my stay, new supplies of fire-wood outside the great Hindu burning ground in Queen's Road; and yet no epidemic was raging; the city was normal save for a strike of mill-hands. It is true that I met wedding parties almost equally often; but in India a wedding party is not, as with us, a suggestion of new life to replace the dead, for the brides so often are infants.

One of the differences between the poor of London and the poor of India may be noticed here. In the East-End a funeral is considered to be a failure unless its cost is out of all proportion to the survivors' means, while a wedding is a matter of a few shillings; whereas in India a funeral is a simple ceremony, to be hurried over, while the wedding festivities last for weeks and often plunge the family into debts from which they never recover.

THE GARLANDS

The selective processes of the memory are very curious. It has been decreed that one of my most vivid recollections of Bombay should be that of the embarrassment and half-amused self-consciousness of an American business man on the platform of the railway station for Delhi. Having completed his negotiatory visit he was being speeded on his way by the native staff of the firm, who had hung him with garlands like a sacrificial bull. In the Crawford Market I had watched the florists at work tearing the blossoms from a kind of frangipani known as the Temple Flower, in order to string them tightly into chains; and now and again in the streets one came upon people wearing them; but to find a shrewd and portly commercial American thus bedecked was a shock. As it happened, he was to share my compartment, and on entering, just before the train started, he apologised very heartily for importing so much heavy perfume into the atmosphere, but begged to be excused because it was the custom of the country and he didn't like to hurt anyone's feelings. He then stood at the door, waving farewells, and directly the line took a bend flung the wreaths out of the window. I was glad of his company, for in addition to these floral offerings his Bombay associates had provided him with a barrel of the best oranges that ever were grown — sufficient for a battalion — and these we consumed at brief intervals all the way to Delhi.

DELHI

"If you can be in India only so short a time as seven weeks," said an artist friend of mine — and among his pictures is a sombre representation of the big sacred bull that grazes under the walls of Delhi Fort — "why not stay in Delhi all the while? You will then learn far more of India than by rushing about." I think he was right, although it was not feasible to accept the advice. For Delhi has so much; it has, first and foremost, the Fort; it has the Jama Masjid, that immense mosque where on Fridays at one o'clock may be seen Mohammedans of every age wearing every hue, thousands worshipping as one; it has the ancient capitals scattered about the country around it; it has signs and memories of the Mutiny; it has delectable English residences; and it has the Chadni Chauk, the long main street with all its curious buildings and crowds and countless tributary alleys, every one of which is the East crystallised, every one of which has its white walls, its decorative doorways, its loiterers, its beggars, its artificers, and its defiance of the bogey, Progress.

Another thing: in January, Delhi, before the sun is high and after he has sunk, is cool and bracing.

But, most of all, Delhi is interesting because it was the very centre of the Mogul dominance, and when one has become immersed in the story of the great rulers, from Babar to Aurungzebe, one thinks of most other history as insipid. Of Babar, who reigned from 1526 to 1530, I saw no trace in India; but his son Humayun (1530-1556) built Indrapat, which is just outside the walls of Delhi, and he lies close by in the beautiful mausoleum that bears his name. Humayun's son, Akbar (1556-1605), preferred Agra to Delhi; nor was Jahangir (1605-1627), who succeeded Akbar, a great builder hereabout; but with Shah Jahan (1627-1658), Jahangir's son, came the present Delhi's golden age. He it was who built the Jama Masjid, the great mosque set commandingly on a mound and gained by magnificent flights of steps. To the traveller approaching the city from any direction the two graceful minarets of the mosque stand for Delhi. It was Shah Jahan, price of Mogul builders, who decreed also the palace in the Fort, to say nothing (at the moment) of the Taj Mahal at Agra; while two of his daughters, Jahanara, and Roshanara, that naughty Begam, enriched Delhi too, the little pavilion in the Gardens that bear Roshanara's name being a gem. Wandering among these architectural delights, now empty and under alien protection, it is difficult to believe that their period was as recent as Cromwell and Milton. But in India the sense of chronology vanishes.

After Shah Jahan came his crafty son, Aurungzebe, who succeeded in keeping his empire together until 1707, and with him the grandeur of the Grand Moguls waned and after him ceased to be, although not until the Mutiny was their rule extinguished. As I have just said, in India the sense of chronology vanishes, or goes astray, and it is with a start that one is confronted, in the Museum in Delhi Fort, by a photograph of the last Mogul!

In Bombay, during my wakeful moments in the hottest part of the day, I had passed the time and imbibed instruction by reading the three delightful books of the late E. H. Aitken, who called himself "Eha" — "Behind the Bungalow," "The Tribes on My Frontier" and "A Naturalist on the Prowl." No more amusing and kindly studies of the fauna, flora and human inhabitants of a country can have ever been written than these; and I can suggest, to the domestically curious mind, no better preparation for a visit to India. But at Raisina, when the cool evenings set in and it was pleasant to get near the wood fire, I took to history and revelled in the story of the Moguls as told by many authorities, but most entertainingly perhaps by Tavernier, the French adventurer who took service under Aurungzebe. If any one wants to know what Delhi was like in the seventeenth century during Aurungzebe's long reign, and how the daily life in the Palace went, and would learn more of the power and autocracy and splendour and cruelty of the Grand Moguls, let him get Tavernier's record. If once I began to quote from it I should never stop; and therefore I pass on, merely remarking that when you have finished the travels of M. Tavernier, the travels of M. Bernier, another contemporary French observer, await you. And I hold you to be envied.

The Palace in the Fort is now but a fraction of what it was in the time of Aurungzebe and his father, but enough remains to enable the imaginative mind to reconstruct the past, especially if one has read my two annalists. One of Bernier's most vivid passages describes the Diwan- i-Am, or Hall of Public Audience, the building to which, after leaving the modern military part of the Fort, one first comes, where the Moguls sat in state during a durbar, and painted and gilded elephants, richly draped, took part in the obeisances. Next comes the Hall of Private Audiences, where the Peacock Throne once stood. It has now vanished, but in its day it was one of the wonders of the world, the tails of the two guardian peacocks being composed of precious stones and the throne itself being of jewelled gold. It was for this that one of Shah Jahan's poets wrote an inscription in which we find such lines as —

By the order of the Emperor the azure of Heaven was exhausted on its decoration....

The world had become so short of gold on account of its use
in the throne that the purse of the Earth was empty of treasure....

On a dark night, by the lustre of its rubies and pearls it can
lend stars to a hundred skies....

That was right enough, no doubt, but when our poet went on to
say,

As long as a trace remains of existence and space
Shah Jahan shall continue to sit on this throne,

we feel that he was unwise. Such pronouncements can be tested.
As it happened, Shah Jahan was destined, very shortly after the
poem was written, to be removed into captivity by his son, and the
rest of his unhappy life was spent in a prison at Agra. On each end
wall of the Hall of Private Audience is the famous couplet, —

If there is a Paradise on the face of the earth,
It is this, Oh! it is this, Oh! it is this.

I think of the garden and palace of Delhi Fort as the loveliest spot
in India. Not the most beautiful, not the most impressive; but the
loveliest. The Taj Mahal has a greater beauty; the ruined city of
Fatehpur-Sikri has a greater dignity; but for the perfection of domestic regality in design and material and workmanship, this marble home and mosque and accompanying garden and terrace could
not be excelled. After the Halls of Audience we come to the seraglio
and accompanying buildings, where everything is perfect and nothing is on the grand scale. The Pearl Mosque could hardly be smaller;
and it is as pure and fresh as a lotus. There is a series of apartments
all in white marble (with inlayings of gold and the most delicately
pierced marble gratings) through which a stream of water used to
run (and it ran again at the Coronation Durbar in 1911, when the
Royal Baths were again made to "function") that must be one of the
most magical of the works of man. Every inch is charming and distinguished. All these rooms are built along the high wall which in

the time of Shah Jahan and his many lady loves was washed by the Jumna. But to-day the river has receded and a broad strip of grass intervenes.

A DAY'S HAWKING

One of my best Indian days was that on which Colonel Sir Umar Hayat Khan took us out a-hawking. Sir Umar is himself something of a hawk—an impressive figure in his great turban with long streamers, his keen aquiline features and blackest of hair. All sport comes naturally to him, whether hunting or shooting, pig-sticking, coursing or falconry; and the Great War found him with a sports-man's eagerness to rush into the fray, where he distinguished him-self notably.

We found this gallant chieftain in the midst of his retainers on the further bank of the Jumna, at the end of the long bridge. Here the plains begin—miles of fields of stubble, with here and there a tree and here and there a pool or marsh, as far as eye can reach, an an-cient walled city in the near distance being almost the only excres-cence. Between the river and this city was our hunting ground.

With the exception of Sir Umar, two of his friends and ourselves, the company was on foot; and nothing more like the middle ages did I ever see. The retainers were in every kind of costume, one having an old pink coat and one a green; one leading a couple of greyhounds in case we put up a hare; others carrying guns (for we were prepared for all); while the chief falconer and his assistants had their hawks on their wrists, and one odd old fellow was pro-vided with a net, in which a captive live hawk was to flutter and struggle to attract his hereditary foes, the little birds, who, deeming him unable to hit back, were to swarm down to deride and defy and be caught in the meshes.

I may say at once that hawking, particularly in this form, does not give me much pleasure. There is something magnificent in the flight of the falcon when it is released and flung towards its prey, but the odds are too heavy in its favour and the whimperings of the doomed quarry strike a chill in the heart. We flew our hawks at duck and plovers, and missed none. Often the first swoop failed, but the deadly implacable pursuer was instantly ready to swoop again, and rarely was a third manoeuvre necessary. Man, under the influence of the excitement of the chase, is the same all the world over, and there was no difference between these Indians moving swiftly to intervene between the hawk and its stricken prey and an English boy running to retrieve his rabbit. Their animation and triumph—even their shouts and cries—were alike.

And so we crossed field after field on our gentle steeds—and no one admires gentleness in a horse more than I—stopping only to watch another tragedy of the air, or to look across the river to Delhi and see the Fort under new conditions. All this country I had so often looked down upon from those high massive walls, standing in one of the lovely windows of Shah Jahan's earthly paradise; and now the scene was reversed, and I began to take more delight in it than in the sport. But at a pond to which we next came there was enacted a drama so absorbing that everything else was forgotten, even the heat of the sun.

Upon this pond were three wild-duck at which a falcon was instantly flown. For a while, however, they kept their presence of mind and refused to leave the water—diving beneath the surface at the moment that the enemy was within a foot of them. On went the hawk, in its terrible, cruel onset, and up came the ducks, all ready to repeat these tactics when it turned and attacked again. But on one of the party (I swear it was not I), in order to assist the hawk, firing his gun, two of the ducks became panic-stricken and left the water, only of course to be quickly destroyed. It was on the hawk's return journey to the pond to make sure of the third duck that I saw for the first time in my life— and I hope the last—the expression on the countenance of these terrible birds in the execution of their duty: more than the mere execution of duty, the determination to have no more nonsense, to put an end to anything so monstrous as self-protection in others; for my horse being directly in the way, he flew under its neck and for a moment I thought that he was confusing me with the desired mallard. Nothing more merciless or purposeful did I ever see.

Then began a really heroic struggle on the part of the victim. He timed his dives to perfection, and escaped so often that the spirit of chivalry would have decreed a truce. But blood had been tasted, and, the desire being for more, the guns were again discharged. Not even they, however, could divert the duck from his intention of saving his life, and he dived away from the shot, too.

It was at this moment that assistance to the gallant little bird arrived—not from man, who was past all decency, but from brother feathers. Out of a clear sky suddenly appeared two tern, dazzling in their whiteness, and these did all in their power to infuriate the hawk and lure him from the water. They flew round him and over him; they called him names; they said he was a bully and that all of us (which was true) ought to be ashamed of ourselves; they daunted and challenged and attacked. But the enemy was too strong for them. A fusillade drove them off, and once again we were free to consider the case of the duck, who was still swimming anxiously about, hoping against hope. More shots were fired, one of the boys waded in with a stick, and the dogs were added to the assault; and in the face of so determined a bombardment the poor little creature at last flew up, to be struck down within a few seconds by the insatiable avenger.

That was the crowning event of the afternoon. Thereafter we had only small successes, and some very pronounced failures when, as happened several times, a bird flew for safety through a tree, and the hawk, following, was held up amid the branches. One of the birds thus to escape was a blue jay of brilliant beauty. We also got some hares. And then we loitered back under the yellowing sky, and Sir Umar Hayat Khan ceased suddenly to be a foe of fur and feathers and became a poet, talking of sunsets in India and in England as though the appreciation of tender beauty were his only delight.

NEW, OR IMPERIAL, DELHI

There have been seven Delhis; and it required no little courage to establish a new one — the Imperial capital — actually within sight of most of them; but the courage was forthcoming. Originally the position was to be to the north of the present city, where the Coronation Durbar spread its canvas, but Raisina was found to be healthier, and it is there, some five miles to the south-west, that the new palaces are rising from the rock. Fatehpur-Sikri is the only city with which the New Delhi can be compared; but not Akbar himself could devise it on a nobler scale. Akbar's centralising gift and Napoleon's spacious views may be said to combine here, the long avenues having kinship with the Champs Elysées, and Government House and the Secretariat on the great rocky plateau at Raisina corresponding to the palace on Fatehpur-Sikri's highest point. The splendour and the imagination which designed the lay-out of Imperial Delhi cannot be over-praised, and under the hands of Sir Edwin Lutyens and Mr. Herbert Baker some wonderful buildings are coming to life. The city, since it is several square miles in extent, cannot be finished for some years, but it may be ready to be the seat of Government as soon as 1924.

As I have said, the old Delhis are all about the new one. On the Grand Trunk road out of Delhi proper, which goes to Muttra and Agra, you pass, very quickly, on the left, the remains of Firozabad, the capital of Firoz Shah in the later thirteenth century. Two or three miles further on is Indrapat on its hill overlooking the Jumna, surrounded by lofty walls. It is as modern as the sixteenth century, but is now in ruins. At Indrapat reigned Humayun, the son of the mighty Babar (who on his conquering way to Delhi had swum every river in advance of his army) and the father of the mighty Akbar. I loitered long within Indrapat's massive walls, which are now given up to a few attendants and an occasional visitor, and like all the monuments around Delhi are most carefully conserved under the Act for that purpose, which was not the least of Lord Curzon's Viceregal achievements. Among the buildings which still stand, rising from the turf, is Humayun's library. It was here that he met his end — one tradition relating that he fell in the dark on his way to fetch a book, and another that his purpose had been less intellectually amatory.

Another mile and we come, still just beside the Grand Trunk road, to Humayun's Tomb, which stands in a vast garden where green parrots continually chatter and pursue each other. There is something very charming — a touch of the truest civilisation, if civilisation means the art of living graciously — in the practice of the old Emperors and rulers, of building their mausoleums during their lifetime and using them, until their ultimate destiny was fulfilled, as pleasure resorts. To this enchanting spot came Humayun and his ladies full of life, to be insouciant and gay. Then, his hour striking, Humayun's happy retreat became Humayun's Tomb. He died in 1556, when Queen Mary, in England, was persecuting Protestants. The Tomb is in good repair and to the stranger to the East who has not yet visited Agra and seen the Taj Mahal (which has a similar ground plan), it is as beautiful as need be. Humayun's cenotaph, in plain white marble, is in the very centre. Below, in the vault immediately beneath it, are his remains. Other illustrious dust is here, too; and some less illustrious, such as that of Humayun's barber, which reposes beneath a dome of burning-blue tiles in a corner of the garden.

From the upper galleries of the Emperor's mausoleum the eye enjoys various rich prospects — the valley of the Jumna pulsating in the heat, the walls of the New Delhi at Raisina almost visibly growing, and, to the north, Delhi itself, with the twin towers of the great mosque over all. Down the Grand Trunk road, immediately below, are bullock wagons and wayfarers, and here and there is a loaded camel. Across the road is a curious little group of sacred buildings whither some of the wayfarers no doubt are bent on a pilgrimage; for here is the shrine of the Saint Nizam-ud-din Aulia, who worked miracles during his life and died during the reign of our Edward II — in 1324.

On visiting his shrine (which involved the usual assumption of overshoes to prevent our infidel leather from contaminating the floor), we fell, after evading countless beggars and would-be guides, into the hands of a kindly old man who pressed handfuls of little white nuts upon us and who remains in my memory as the only independent Mussulman priest in India, for he refused a tip. In this respect nothing could be more widely separated than his conduct and that of the three priests of the Jama Masjid in Delhi, who, discovering us on the wall, just before the Friday service began, held up the service for several minutes while they explained their schedule of gratuities—beginning with ten rupees for the High Priest—and this after we had already provided for the attendant who had supplied the overshoes and had led us to the point of vantage! I thought how amusing it would be if a visitor to an English cathedral—where money usually has to pass, as it is—were surrounded by the Dean, Archdeacon, Canons and Minor Canons, with outstretched hands, and had to buy his way to a sight of the altar, according to the status of each. The spectacle would be as odd to us, as it must be to the French or Italians—and even perhaps Americans—to see a demand for an entrance fee on the Canterbury portals.

Were we to continue on the Grand Trunk road for a few miles, first crossing a noble Mogul bridge, we should come to a little walled city, Badapur, where a turning due west leads to another Delhi of the past, Tughlakabad, and on to yet another, the remains of Lal Kot, where the famous Minar soars to the sky.

One of the most pleasing effects of the New Delhi is the series of vistas which the lay-out provides. It has been so arranged that many of the avenues radiating from the central rock on which Government House and the Secretariat are being set are closed at their distant ends by historic buildings. Standing on the temporary tower which marks this centre one is able to see in a few moments all the ruined cities that I have mentioned. The Kutb Minar is the most important landmark in the far south, although the eye rests most lovingly on the red and white comeliness of the tomb of Safdar Jang in the middle distance—which, with Humayun's Tomb, makes a triangle with the new Government House. Within that triangle are the Lodi tombs, marking yet another period in the history of Delhi, the Lodis being the rulers who early in the fifteenth century were defeated by Babar.

The Kutb Minar enclosure, which is a large garden, where beautiful masonry, flowers, trees and birds equally flourish, commemorates the capture of Delhi by Muhammad bin Sam in 1193, the battle being directed by his lieutenant, Kutb-ud-din. From that time until the Mutiny in 1857 Delhi was under Mohammedan rule. One of the first acts of the conqueror was to destroy the Hindu temple that stood here and erect the mosque that now takes its place, and he then built the great tower known as the Kutb Minar, or Tower of Victory, which ascends in diminishing red and white storeys to a height of 235 feet, involving the inquisitive view- finder in a climb of 379 steps. On the other side of the mosque are the beginnings of a second tower, which, judging by the size of the base, was to have risen to a still greater height, but it was abandoned after 150 feet. Its purpose was to celebrate for ever the glory of the Emperor Ala-ud-din (1296-1316).

In front of the mosque is the Iron Pillar which has been the cause of so much perplexity both to antiquaries and chemists, and meat and drink to Sanscrit scholars. The pillar has an inscription commemorating an early monarch named Chandra who conquered Bengal in the fifth century, and it must have been brought to this spot for re-erection. But its refusal to rust, and the purity of its constituents, are its special merits. To me the mysteries of iron pillars are without interest, and what I chiefly remember of this remarkable pleasaunce is the exquisite stone carvings of the ruined cloisters and the green parrots that play among the trees.

THE DIVERS

As we were leaving the Kutb after a late afternoon visit, my host and I were hailed excitedly by an elderly man whose speech was incomprehensible, but whose gestures indicated plainly enough that there was something important up the hill. The line of least resistance being the natural one in India, we allowed him to guide us, and came after a few minutes, among the ruins of the citadel of Lal Kot, to one of those deep wells gained by long flights of steps whither the ladies of the palaces used to resort in the hottest weather. Evening was drawing on and the profundities of this cavern were forbiddingly gloomy; nor was the scene rendered more alluring by the presence of three white-bearded old men, almost stark naked and leaner than greyhounds, who shivered and grimaced, and suggested nothing so much as fugitives from the grave. They were, however, not only alive, but athletically so, being professional divers who earned an exceedingly uncomfortable living by dropping, feet first, from the highest point of the building into the water eighty feet below.

One of them indicating his willingness—more than willingness, eagerness—to perform this manoeuvre for two rupees, we agreed, and placing us on a step from which the best view could be had, he fled along the gallery to the top of the shaft, and after certain preliminary movements, to indicate how perilous was the adventure, and how chilly the evening, and how more than worth two rupees it was, he committed his body to the operations of the law of gravity. We saw it through the apertures in the shaft on its downward way and then heard the splash as it reached the distant water, while a crowd of pigeons who had retired to roost among the masonry dashed out and away. The diver emerged from the well and came running up the steps towards us, while his companion scarecrows fled also to the top of the shaft and one after the other dropped down, too; so that in a minute or so we were surrounded by three old, dripping men, each demanding two rupees. Useless to protest that we had desired but one of them to perform: they pursued us into the open, and even clung to our knees, and of course we paid— afterwards to learn that one rupee for the lot was a lavish guerdon.

One meets with these divers continually, wherever there is a pool sacred or otherwise; but some actually leap into the water and do not merely drop. At the shrine of the Saint Nizam-ud-din, near Humayun's Tomb, I found them—but there they were healthy-looking youths—and again at Fatehpur-Sikri. But for this sporadic diving, the wrestling bouts which are common everywhere, the Nautch and the jugglers, India seems to have no pastimes.

THE ROPE TRICK

The returning traveller from India is besieged by questioners who want to know all about the most famous of the jugglers' performances. In this trick the magician flings a rope into the air, retaining one end in his hand, and his boy climbs up it and disappears. I did not see it.

AGRA AND FATEHPUR-SIKRI

All the Indian cities that I saw seemed to cover an immense acreage, partly because every modern house has its garden and compound. In a country where land is cheap and servants are legion there need be no congestion, and, so far, the Anglo-Indian knows little or nothing of the embarrassments of dwellers in New York or London. To every one in India falls naturally a little faithful company of assistants to oil the wheels of life — groom, gardener, butler and so forth — and a spacious dwelling-place to think of England in, and calculate the variable value of the rupee, and wonder why the dickens So-and-so got his knighthood. Agra seemed to me to be the most widespreading city of all; but very likely it is not. In itself it is far from being the most interesting, but it has one building of great beauty — the Pearl Mosque in the Fort — and one building of such consummate beauty as to make it a place of pilgrimage that no traveller would dare to avoid — the Taj Mahal. Whether or not the Taj Mahal is the most enchanting work of architecture in the world I leave it to more extensive travellers to say. To my eyes it has an unearthly loveliness which I make no effort to pass on to others.

The Taj Mahal was built by that inspired friend of architecture, Shah Jahan, as the tomb of the best beloved of his wives, Arjmand Banu, called Mumtaz-i-Mahal or Pride of the Palace. There she lies, and there lies her husband. I wonder how many of the travellers who stand entranced before this mausoleum, in sunshine and at dusk or under the moon, and who have not troubled about its history, realise that Giotto's Tower in Florence is three centuries older, and St. Peter's in Rome antedates it by a little, and St. Paul's Cathedral in London is only twenty or thirty years younger. Yet so it is. In India one falls naturally into the way of thinking of everything that is not of our own time as being of immense age, if not prehistoric.

Opinions differ as to the respective beauties of Agra Fort and Delhi Fort, but in so far as the enclosures themselves are considered I give my vote unhesitatingly to Delhi. Yet when one thinks also of what can be seen from the ramparts, then the palm goes instantly to Agra, for its view of the Taj Mahal. It is tragic, walking here, to think of the last days of Shah Jahan, who brought into being both the marble palace and the wonderful Moti-Masjid or marble mosque. For in 1658 his son, Aurungzebe, deposed him and for the rest of his life he was imprisoned in these walls.

His grandfather, Akbar, the other great Agra builder, was made of sterner stuff. All Shah Jahan's creations—the Taj, the marble mosque, the palaces both here and at Delhi, even the great Jama Masjid at Delhi,—have a certain sensuous quality. They are not exactly decadent, but they suggest sweetness rather than strength. The Empire had been won, and Shah Jahan could indulge in luxury and ease. But Akbar had had to fight, and he remained to the end a man of action, and we see his character reflected in his stronghold Fatehpur-Sikri, which one visits from Agra and never forgets. If I were asked to say which place in India most fascinated me and touched the imagination I think I should name this dead city.

Akbar, the son of Babar, is my hero among the Moguls, and this was Akbar's chosen home, until scarcity of water forced him to abandon it for Agra. Akbar, the noblest of the great line of Moguls whose splendour ended in 1707 with the death of Aurungzebe, came to the throne in 1556, only eight years before Shakespeare was born, and died in 1605, and it is interesting to realise how recent were his times, the whole suggestion of Fatehpur-Sikri being one of very remote antiquity. Yet when it was being built so modern a masterpiece as *Hamlet* was being written and played. Those interested in the Great Moguls ought really to visit Fatehpur-Sikri before Delhi or Agra, because Akbar was the grandfather of Shah Jahan.

But there can be no such chronological wanderings in India. Have we not already seen Humayun's Tomb, outside Delhi?—and Humayun was Akbar's father.

They say the leopard and the jackal keep
The courts where Akbar gloried….

—this adaptation of FitzGerald's lines ran through my mind as we passed from room to room and tower to tower of Fatehpur-Sikri. There is nothing to compare with it, except perhaps Pompeii. And in that comparison one realises how impossible it is at a hazard to date an Indian ruin, for, as I have said, Fatehpur-Sikri is from the days of Elizabeth, while Pompeii was destroyed in the first century, and yet Pompeii in many ways seems less ancient.

The walls of Fatehpur-Sikri are seven miles round and the city rises to the summits of two steep hills. It was on the higher one that Akbar set his palace. Civilisation has run a railway through the lower levels; the old high road still climbs the hill under the incredibly lofty walls of the palace. The royal enclosure is divided into all the usual courtyards and apartments, but they are on a grander scale. Also the architecture is more mixed. Here is the swimming bath; here are the cool, dark rooms for the ladies of the harem in the hottest days, with odd corners where Akbar is said to have played hide-and-seek with them; here is the hall where Akbar, who kept an open mind on religion, listened to, and disputed with, dialecticians of varying creeds—himself seated in the middle, and the doctrinaires in four pulpits around him; here is the Mint; here is the house of the Turkish queen, with its elaborate carvings and decorations; here is the girls' school, with a courtyard laid out for human chess, the pieces being slave-girls; here is a noble mosque; here is the vast court where the great father of his people administered justice, or what approximated to it, and received homage. Here are the spreading stables and riding school; here is even the tomb of a favourite elephant.

And here is the marble tomb of the Saint, the Shaikh Salim, whose holiness brought it about that the Emperor became at last the father of a son—none other than Jahangir. The shrine is visited even to this day by childless wives, who tie shreds of their clothing to the lattice-work of a marble window as an earnest of their maternal worthiness. It is visited also by the devout for various purposes, among others by those whose horses are sick and who nail votive horseshoes to the great gate. According to tradition the mother of Jahangir was a Christian named Miriam, and her house and garden may be seen, the house having the traces of a fresco which by those who greatly wish it can be believed to represent the Annunciation. Tradition, however, is probably wrong, and the princess was from Jaipur and a true Mussulwoman.

From every height—and particularly from the Panch Mahal's roof—one sees immense prospects and realises what a landmark the stronghold of Fatehpur-Sikri must have been to the dwellers in the plains; but no view is the equal of that which bursts on the astonished eyes at the great north gateway, where all Rajputana is at one's feet. I do not pretend to any exhaustive knowledge of the gates of the world, but I cannot believe that there can be others set as this Gate of Victory is in the walls of a palace, at the head of myriad steps, on the very top of a commanding rock and opening on to thousands of square miles of country. Having seen the amazing landscape one descends the steps to the road, and looking up is astonished and exalted by seeing the gate from below. Nothing so grand has ever come into my ken. The Taj Mahal is unforgettingly beautiful; but this glorious gate in the sky has more at once to exercise and stimulate the imagination and reward the vision.

On the gate are the words: "Isa (Jesus), on whom be peace, said: 'The world is a bridge; pass over it, but build no house on it. The world endures but an hour; spend it in devotion.'"

Having seen Fatehpur-Sikri, where Akbar lived and did more than build a house, it is a natural course to return to Agra by way of Sikandra, where he was buried. Sikandra is like the Taj Mahal and Humayun's Tomb in general disposition—the mausoleum itself being in the centre of a garden. But it is informed by a more sombre spirit. The burial-place of the mighty Emperor is in the very heart of the building, gained by a sloping passage lit by an attendant with a torch. Here was Akbar laid, while high above, on the topmost stage of the mausoleum, in the full light, is his cenotoph of marble, with the ninety-nine names of Allah inscribed upon it. Near the cenotaph is a marble pillar on which once was set the Koh-i-noor diamond, chief of Akbar's treasures. To-day it is part of the English regalia.

LUCKNOW

The Ridge at Delhi is a sufficiently moving reminder of the Indian Mutiny; but it is at Lucknow that the most poignant phases are re-enacted. At Delhi may be seen, preserved for ever, the famous buildings which the British succeeded in keeping—Hindu Rao's house, and the Observatory, and Flagstaff Tower, the holding of which gave them victory; while in the walls of the Kashmir Gate our cannon balls are still visibly imbedded. There is also the statue of John Nicholson in the Kudsia Garden, and in the little Museum of the Fort are countless souvenirs.

But Lucknow was the centre of the tragedy, and the Residency is preserved as a sacred spot. Not even the recent Great War left in its track any more poignant souvenirs of fortitude and disaster than the little burial ground here, around the ruins of the church, where those who fell in the Mutiny and those who fought or suffered in the Mutiny are lying. Long ago as it was—1857—there are still a few vacant lots destined to be filled. Chief of the tombstones that bear the honoured names is that of the heroic defender who kept upon the topmost roof the banner of England flying. It has the simple and touching inscription: "Here lies Henry Lawrence, who tried to do his duty. May the Lord have mercy on his soul!"

In the Residency every step of the siege and relief can be followed. I was there first on a serene evening after rain; and but for some tropical trees it might have been an English scene. All that was lacking was a thrush or blackbird's note; but the grass was as soft and green as at home and the air as sweet. I shall long retain the memory of the contrast between the incidents which give this enclosure its unique place in history and the perfect calm brooding over all. And whenever any one calls my attention to a Bougainvillaea I shall say, "Ah! But you should see the Bougainvillaea in the Residency garden at Lucknow."

Everywhere that I went in India I found this noble lavish shrub in full flower, but never wearing such a purple as at Lucknow. The next best was in the Fort at Delhi. It was not till I reached Calcutta that I caught any glimpse of the famous scarlet goldmore tree in leaf; but I saw enough to realise how splendid must be the effect of an avenue of them. Bombay, however, was rich in hedges of poinsettia, and they serve as an introduction to the goldmore's glory.

Before leaving the Residency I should like to quote a passage from the little brochure on the defence of Lucknow which Sir Harcourt Butler, the Governor of the United Provinces, with characteristic thoughtfulness has prepared for the use of his guests. "The visitor to the Residency," he wrote, thinking evidently of a similar evening to that on which we visited it, "who muses on the past and the future, may note that upon the spot where the enemy's assault was hottest twin hospitals for Europeans and Indians have been erected by Oudh's premier Taluqdar, the Maharaja of Balrampur; and as the sun sets over the great city, lingering awhile on the trim lawns and battered walls which link the present with the past, a strong hope may come to him, like a distant call to prayer, that old wounds may soon be healed, and old causes of disunion may disappear, and that Englishmen and Indians, knit together by loyalty to their beloved Sovereign, may be as brothers before the altar of the Empire, bearing the Empire's burden, and sharing its inestimable privileges, and, it may be, adding something not yet seen or dreamt of to its worldwide and weather-beaten fame."

I left Lucknow with regret, and would advise any European with time to spare, and the desire to be at once civilised and warm, to think seriously of spending a winter there instead of in the illusory sunshine of the Riviera, or the comparative barbarity of Algiers. The journey is longer, but the charm of the place would repay.

A TIGER

To have the opportunity of hunting a tiger—on an elephant too—which by a stroke of luck fell to me, is to experience the un-English character of India at its fullest. Almost everything else could be reproduced elsewhere—the palaces, the bazaars, the caravans, the mosques and temples with their worshippers—but not the jungle, the Himalayas, the vast swamps through which our elephants waded up to the Plimsoll, the almost too painful ecstasies of the pursuit of an eater of man.

The master of the chase, who has many tigers to his name, was Sir Harcourt Butler, whose hospitality is famous, so large and warm is it, and so minute, and it was because he was not satisfied that the ordinary diversions of the "Lucknow Week" were sufficient for his guests, that he impulsively arranged a day's swamp-deer shooting on the borders of Nepaul. The time was short, or of elephants there would have been seventy or more; as it was, we were apologised to (there were only about six of us) for the poverty of the supply, a mere five and twenty being obtainable. But to these eyes, which had never seen more than six elephants at once, and those in the captivity either of a zoo or a circus, a row of five and twenty was astounding. They were waiting for us on the plain, at a spot distant some score of miles by car, through improvised roads, from the station, whither an all-night railway journey had borne us. The name of the station, if I ever knew it, I have forgotten: there was no room in my heated brain for such trifles; but I have forgotten nothing else.

It was after an hour and a half's drive in the cool and spicy early morning air—between the fluttering rags on canes which told the drivers how to steer—that we came suddenly in sight of some distant tents and beside them an immense long dark inexplicable mass which through the haze seemed now and then to move. As we drew nearer, this mass was discerned to be a row of elephants assembled in line ready to salute the Governor. The effect was more impressive and more Eastern than anything I had seen. Grotesque too—for some had painted faces and gilded toes, and not a few surveyed me with an expression in which the comic spirit was too noticeable. Six or seven had howdahs, the rest blankets: those with howdahs being for the party and its leader, Bam Bahadur, a noted shikaree; and the others to carry provisions and bring back the spoil. On the neck of each sat an impassive mahout.

To one to whom the pen is mightier than the gun and whose half a century's bag contains only a few rabbits, a hedgehog and a moorhen, it is no inconsiderable ordeal to be handed a repeating rifle and some dozens of cartridges and be told that that is your elephant—the big one there, with the red ochre on its forehead. To be on an elephant in the jungle without the responsibilities of a lethal weapon would be sufficient thrill for one day: but to be expected also to deal out death was too much. In the company of others, however, one can do anything; and I gradually ascended to the top, not, as the accomplished hunters did, by placing a foot on the trunk and being swung heavenwards, but painfully, on a ladder; by my side being a very keen Indian youth, the son of a minor chieftain, who spoke English perfectly and was to instruct me in Nimrod's lore.

And so the procession started, and for a while discomfort set acutely in, for the movement of a howdah is short and jerky, and it takes some time both to adjust oneself to it and to lose the feeling that the elephant sooner or later—and probably sooner—must trip and fall. But the glory of the morning, the urgency of our progress, the novelty and sublimity of the means of transport, the strangeness of the scene, and my companion's speculations on the day's promise, overcame any personal want of ease and I forgot myself in the universal. Our destination was a series of marshes some six miles away, where the gonds—or swamp-deer— were usually found, and we were divided up, some elephants, of which mine was one, taking the left wing, with instructions on reaching a certain spot to wait there for the deer who would move off in that direction; others taking the right wing; and others beating up the middle.

We began with a trial of nervous stamina—for a river far down in its bed below us almost immediately occurred, and this had to be crossed. I abandoned all hope as the elephant descended the bank almost, as it seemed, perpendicularly, and plunged into the water with an enormous splash. But after he had squeeged through, extricating himself with a gigantic wrench, the ground was level for a long while, and there was time to look around and recollect one's fatalism. Far ahead in a blue mist were the Himalayas. All about were unending fields, with here and there white cattle grazing. Cranes stretched their necks above the grass; now and then a herd of blackbuck (which were below our hunting ambitions) scampered away; the sky was full of wild-duck and other water-fowl.

Of the hunting of the gond I should have something to say had not a diversion occurred which relegated that lively and elusive creature to an obscure place in the background. We had finished the beat, and most of us had emerged from the swamp to higher ground where an open space, or maidan, corresponding to a drive in an English preserve, but on the grand scale, divided it from the jungle—all our thoughts being set upon lunch—when suddenly across this open space passed a blur of yellow and black only a few yards from the nearest elephant. It was so unexpected and so quick that even the trained eyes of my companion were uncertain. "Did you see?" he asked me in a voice of hushed and wondering awe. "Could that have been a tiger?" I could not say, but I understood his excitement. For the tiger is the king of Indian carnivorae, the most desired of all game. Hunters date their lives by them: such and such a thing happened not on the anniversary of their wedding day; not when their boy went to Balliol; not when they received the K.C.I.E.; but in the year that they shot this or that man-eater.

That a tiger had really chanced upon us we soon ascertained. Also that it had been hit by the rifle on the first elephant and had disappeared into the jungle, which consisted hereabouts of a grass some twenty feet high, bleached by the sun.

A Council of War followed, and we were led by Bam Bahadur on a rounding- up manoeuvre. According to his judgment the tiger would remain just inside the cover, and our duty was therefore to make a wide detour and then advance in as solid a semicircle as possible upon him and force him again into the open, where the hunter who had inflicted the first wound was to remain stationed. Accordingly all the rest of us entered the jungle in single file, our elephants treading down the grass with their great irresistible feet or wrenching it away with their invincible trunks. It was now that the shikaree was feeling the elephant shortage. Had there been seventy-five instead of only twenty-five, he said, all would be well: he could then form a cordon such as no tiger might break through. For lack of these others, when the time came to turn and advance upon our prey he caused fires to be lighted here and there where the gaps were widest, so that we forged onwards not only to the accompaniment of the shrill cries of the mahouts and the noise of plunging and overwhelming elephants, but to the fierce roar and crackle of burning stalks.

And thus, after an hour in this bewildering tangle, with the universe filled with sound and strangeness, and the scent of wood smoke mingling with the heat of the air, and the lust of the chase in our veins, we drew to the spot where the animal was guessed to be hiding, and knew that the guess was true by the demeanour of the elephants. Real danger had suddenly entered into the adventure; and they showed it. A wounded tiger at bay can do desperate things, and some of the elephants now refused to budge forward any more, or complied only with terrified screams. Some of the unarmed mahouts were also reluctant, and shouted their fears. But the shikaree was inexorable. There the tiger was, and we must drive it out.

Closer and closer we drew, until every elephant's flank was pressing against its neighbour, the outside ones being each at the edge of the open space; in the middle of which was the twenty-fifth with its vigilant rider standing tense with his rifle to his shoulder. The noise was now deafening. Every one was uttering something, either to scare the tiger or to encourage the elephants or his neighbour or possibly himself; while now and then from the depths of the grass ahead of us came an outraged growl, with more than a suggestion of contempt in it for such unsportsmanship as could array twenty-five elephants, half a hundred men and a dozen rifles against one inoffensive wild beast.

And then suddenly the grass waved, there was a rustle and rush and a snarl of furious rage, and once again a blur of yellow and black crossed the open space. Six or more reports rang out, and to my dying day I shall remember, with mixed feelings, that one of these reports was the result of pressure on a trigger applied by a finger belonging to me. That the tiger was hit again—by other bullets than mine—was certain, but instead of falling it disappeared into the jungle on the other side of the maidan, and again we were destined to employ enclosing tactics. It was now intensely hot, but nobody minded; and we were an hour and a half late for lunch, but nobody minded: the chase was all! The phrase "out for blood" had taken on its literal primitive meaning.

The second rounding-up was less simple than the first, because the tiger had more choice of hiding places; but again our shikaree displayed his wonderful intuition, and in about an hour we had ringed the creature in. That this was to be the end was evident from the electrical purposefulness which animated the old hands. The experienced shots were carefully disposed, and my own peace of mind was not increased by the warning "If the tiger leaps on your elephant, don't shoot"—the point being that novices can be very wild with their rifles under such conditions. As the question "What shall I do instead?" was lost in the tumult, the latter stages of this momentous drama were seen by these eyes less steadily and less whole than I could have wished. But I saw the tiger spring, growling, at an elephant removed some four yards from mine, and I saw it driven back by a shot from one of the native hunters. And then when, after another period of anxious expectancy, it emerged again from the undergrowth, and sprang towards our host, I saw him put two bullets into it almost instantaneously; and the beautiful obstinate creature fell, never to rise again.

THE SACRED CITY

The devout Hindu knows in Benares the height of ecstasy: but, if I am typical, the European experiences there both discomfort and inquietude. Nowhere else in India did I feel so foreign, so alien. To be of cool Christian traditions and an Occidental, an inquisitive sightseer among these fervent pilgrims intent upon their pious duties and rapt in exaltation and unthinking inflexible belief, was in itself disconcerting, almost to the point of shame; while the pilgrims were so remarkably of a different world, a different era, that one felt lost.

This, however, is not all. India is never too sanitary, except where the English are in their own strongholds, but Benares—at any rate the parts which the tourist must visit—is least scrupulous in such matters. The canonization of the cow must needs carry a penalty with it, and Benares might be described as a sanctified byre without any labouring Hercules in prospect. Godliness it may have, but cleanliness is very distant. The streets, too, seem to be narrower and more congested than those in any other city; so that it is often embarrassingly difficult to treat the approaching ruminants with the respect due to them. Fortunately they are seldom anything but mild and unaggressive. Part perplexed, part inquisitive, and part contemptuous, they are met everywhere, while in one of the temples in which the unbeliever may (to his great contentment) do no more than stand at the entrance, they are frankly worshipped. In another temple monkeys are revered too, careering about the walls and courtyards and being fed by the curious and the devout.

Holiness is not only the peculiar characteristic of Benares: it is also its staple industry. In the streets there is a shrine at every few feet, while the shops where little lingams are for sale must be numbered by hundreds.

The chief glory of Benares is, however, the Ganges, on one side of which is the teeming sweltering city with its palaces and temples heaped high for two or three miles, and bathers swarming at the river's edge; while the other bank is flat and bare. A watering-place front on the ocean's shore does not end more suddenly and completely. There is nothing that I have seen with which to compare the north bank of the Ganges, with the morning sun on its many-coloured façades and towers, but Venice. As one is rowed slowly down the river it is of Venice that one instinctively thinks. As in Venice, the palaces are of various colours, pink and red and yellow and blue, and the sun has crumbled their façades in the same way. But there is this difference—that over the Benares roofs the monkeys scamper.

Gradually Venice is forgotten as the novel interest of the scene captures one's whole attention. At each of the ghauts (a landing place or steps) variegated masses of pilgrims — no matter how early the hour, and to see them rightly one ought to start quite by six — are making their ablutions and deriving holiness from the yellow tide. You saw them yesterday trudging wearily through the streets, the sacred city at last reached; and here they are in their thousands, brown and glistening. They are of every age: quite old white-bearded men and withered women, meticulously serious in their ritual, and then boys and girls deriving also a little fun from their immersion. Here and there the bathing ghaut is diversified by a burning ghaut, and one may catch a glimpse of the extremities of the corpse twisting among the faggots. Here and there is a boat or raft in which a priest is seated under his umbrella, fishing for souls as men in punts on the Thames fish for roach. And over all is the pitiless sun, hot even now, before breakfast, but soon to be unbearable.

I was not sorry when the voyage ended and we returned to the Maharajah's Guest House for a little repose and refreshment, before visiting the early Buddhist stronghold at Sarnath, the "Deer Park," where the Master first preached his doctrine and whither his five attendants sought a haven after they had forsaken him. Drifting about its ruins and contemplating the glorious capital of the famous Asoka column — all that has been preserved — I found myself murmuring the couplet, —

With a friendly Buddhist priest I seek respite from
  the strife
And manifold anomalies which go to make up life —

but the odds are that even the early Buddhists were not immune.

CALCUTTA

Calcutta and Bombay are strangely different — so different that they can only be contrasted. Bombay, first and foremost, has the sea, and I can think of nothing more lovely than the sunsets that one watches from the lawn of the Yacht Club or from the promenade on Warder Road. Calcutta has no sea—nothing but a very difficult tidal river. Calcutta, again, has no Malabar Hill. But then Bombay has no open space to compare with the Maidan; and for all its crowded bazaars it has no street so diversified and interesting as Harrison Road. It has no Chinatown. Its climate is enervating where that of Calcutta, if not bracing—and no one could call it that—at any rate does not extract every particle of vigour from the European system.

But the special glory of Calcutta is the Maidan, that vast green space which, unlike so many parks, spreads itself at the city's feet. One does not have to seek it: there it is, with room for every one and a race- course and a cricket-ground to boot. And if there is no magic in the evening prospect such as the sea and its ships under the flaming or mysterious enveiling sky can offer to the eye at Bombay, there is a quality of golden richness in the twilight over Calcutta, as seen across the Maidan, through its trees, that is unique. I rejoiced in it daily. This twilight is very brief, but it is exquisite.

It is easier in Calcutta to be suddenly transported to England than in any other Indian city that I visited. There are, it is true, more statues of Lord Curzon than we are accustomed to; but many of the homes are quite English, save for the multitude of servants; Government House, serene and spacious and patrician, is a replica of Kedlestone Hall in Derbyshire: the business buildings within and without are structurally English, and the familiar Scotch accent sounds everywhere; but the illusion is most complete in St. John's Church, that very charming, cool, white and comfortable sanctuary, in the manner of Wren, and in St. Andrew's too. Secluded here, the world shut off, one might as well be in some urban conventicle at home on a sunny August day, as in the glamorous East. St. John's particularly I shall remember: its light, its distinction, its surrounding verdancy.

ROSE AYLMER

Ah, what avails the sceptred race,
  Ah, what the form divine!
What every virtue, every grace!
  Rose Aylmer, all were thine!

Rose Aylmer, whom these wakeful eyes
  May weep, but never see,
A night of memories and sighs
  I consecrate to thee.

One curious task which I set myself in Calcutta was to find Rose Aylmer's grave, for it was there that, in 1800, the mortal part of the lady whom Landor immortalised was buried. But I tried in vain. I walked for hours amid the sombre pyramidal tombs beneath which the Calcutta English used to be laid, among them, in 1815, Thackeray's father, but I found no trace of her whom I sought. I have seen many famous cemeteries, all depressing, from Kensal Green to Genoa, from Rock Creek to Montmartre, but none can approach in its forlorn melancholy the tract of stained and crumbling sarcophagi packed so close as almost to touch each other, in the burial ground off Rawdon Street and Park Street. Let no one establish a monument of cement over me. Any material rather than that!

JOB AND JOE

If I did not find Rose Aylmer's tomb, I found, in St. John's pleasant God's Acre, the comely mausoleum of Job Charnock, and this delighted me, because for how long has been ringing in my ears that line—

"The tall pale widow is mine, Joe, the little brown girl's for
  you."

which I met with so many years ago in "The Light That Failed,"
where the Nilghai sings it to his own music! He got it, he said, from
a tombstone, in a distant land; and the tombstone is now incorpo-
rated with Job Charnock's, the distant land being India; but the
verses I have had to collect elsewhere. I found them in Calcutta, in
my host's library.

Joe was Joseph, or Josiah, Townsend, a pilot of the Ganges, and
tradition has it that he and Job Charnock, who, as an officer of the
East India Company, founded Calcutta in 1690, saved a pretty
young Hindu widow from ascending her husband's funeral pyre
and committing suttee. Tradition states further that Job Charnock
and his bride "lived lovingly for many years and had several children," until in due time she was buried in the mausoleum at St.
John's, where her husband sacrificed a cock on each anniversary of
her death ever after. The story has been examined and found to be
improbable, but Charnock was a bold fellow who might easily have
started many legends; and the poem remains, and if there is a liveli-
er, I should like to know of it. I have been at the agreeable pains of
reconstructing the verses as they were probably written, so that
there are two more than the Nilghai sang. The whole is a very curious haunting ballad, leaving us with the desire to know much more
of the lives of both men—Job Charnock the frontiersman, and Joseph Townsend, "skilful and industrious, a kind father and a useful
friend," who could navigate not only the Ganges but the shifting
Hooghli. Rarely can so much mixed autobiography and romance
have been packed into six stanzas—and here too the adventurous
East and West meet:—

  I've shipped my cable, messmates, I'm dropping down
    with the tide;
  I have my sailing orders while ye at anchor ride,
  And never, on fair June morning, have I put out to sea
  With clearer conscience, or better hope, or heart more light and
free.

An Ashburnham! A Fairfax! Hark how the corslets ring!
Why are the blacksmiths out to-day, beating those men at the
spring?
Ho, Willie, Hob and Cuddie!—bring out your boats amain,
There's a great red pool to swim them o'er, yonder in Deadman's
Lane.

Nay, do not cry, sweet Katie—only a month afloat
And then the ring and the parson, at Fairlight Church, my doat.
The flower-strewn path—the Press Gang! No, I shall never see
Her little grave where the daisies wave in the breeze on Fairlight
Lee.

"Shoulder to shoulder, Joe, my boy, into the crowd like a wedge!
Out with the hangers, messmates, but do not strike with the edge!"
Cries Charnock, "Scatter the faggots! Double that Brahmin in two!
The tall pale widow is mine, Joe, the little brown girl for you."

Young Joe (you're nearing sixty), why is your hide so dark?
Katie had fair soft blue eyes—who blackened yours? Why, hark!
The morning gun! Ho, steady! The arquebuses to me;
I've sounded the Dutch High Admiral's heart as my lead doth
sound the
   sea.

Sounding, sounding the Ganges—floating down with the tide,
Moor me close by Charnock, next to my nut-brown bride.
My blessing to Katie at Fairlight—Howell, my thanks to you—
Steady!—We steer for Heaven through scud drifts cold and blue.

EXIT

I arrived in Bombay on the last day of 1919 and embarked at Calcutta for Japan on the evening of February 17th, seven weeks later. But to embark at Calcutta is not to leave it, for we merely dropped down the river a short distance that night, and for the next day and a half we were in the Hooghli, sounding all the way. It is a difficult river to emerge from; nor do I recommend any one else to travel, as I did, on a boat with a forward deck cargo of two or three hundred goats on the starboard side and half as many monkeys on the port, with a small elephant tethered between and a cage of leopards adjacent. These, the property of an American dealer in wild animals, were intended for sale in the States; all but one of the leopards, which, being lame, he had decided to kill, to provide a "robe" for his wife. Nothing could be more different than the careless aimless activities of the monkeys I had seen among the trees between Agra and Delhi and scampering over the parapets of Benares, all thieves and libertines with a charter, and the restriction of these poor cowering mannikins, overcrowded in their cages, with an abysmal sorrow in their eyes. Many died on the voyage, and I think the Indian Government should look into the question of their export very narrowly.

JAPAN

INTRODUCTORY

I ought not to write about Japan at all, for I was there but three short weeks, and rain or snow fell almost all the time, and I sailed for America on the very day that the cherry blossom festivities began. But— well, there is only one Fujiyama, and it is surpassingly beautiful and satisfying—the perfect mountain—and I should feel contemptible if I did not add my eulogy of it—my gratitude—to all the others.

Since, then, I am to say something of Fuji, let the way be paved.

THE LITTLE LAND

One is immediately struck, on landing at Kobe—and continually after—by the littleness of Japan. The little flimsy houses, the little flimsy shops, the small men, the toylike women, the tiny children, as numerous and like unto each other as the pebbles on the shore—these are everywhere. But although small of stature the Japanese men are often very powerfully built and many of them suggest great strength. They are taking to games, too. While I was in the country baseball was a craze, and boys were practising pitching and catching everywhere, even in the streets of the cities.

Littleness—with which is associated the most delicate detail and elaborate finish—is the mark also of modern Japanese art. In the curiosity shops whatever was massive or largely simple was Chinese. Even the royal palaces at Kyoto are small, the rooms, exquisite as they are, with perfect joinery and ancient paintings, being seldom more than a few feet square, with very low ceilings. I went over two of these palaces, falling into the hands, at each, of English-speaking officials whose ciceronage was touched with a kind of rapture. At the Nijo, especially, was my guide an enthusiast, becoming lyrical over the famous cartoons of the "Wet Heron" and the "Sleeping Sparrows."

In India I had grown accustomed to removing my shoes at the threshold of mosques. There it was out of deference to Allah, but in Japan the concession is demanded solely in the interests of floor polish, and you take your shoes off not only in palaces and houses but in some of the shops. It gave one an odd burglarious feeling to be creeping noiselessly from room to room of the Nijo; but there was nothing to steal. The place was empty, save for decoration.

There is a certain amplitude in some of the larger Kyoto temples, with their long galleries and massive gateways, but these only serve to accentuate the littleness elsewhere. In the principal Kyoto temple I had for guide a minute Japanese with the ecstatic passion for trifles that seems to mark his race. A picture representing the miracle of the "Fly- away Sparrows," as he called them, was the treasure on which he concentrated, and next to that he drew my attention to the boards of the gangway uniting two buildings, which, as one stepped on them, emitted a sound that the Japanese believe to resemble the song of Philomela. To me it brought no such memory, and the fact that this effect, common in Japan, is technically known as "a nightingale squeak," perhaps supports my insensitiveness.

If old Japan is to be found anywhere it is in Kyoto—in spite of its huge factory chimneys. In Tokio, complete European dress is common in the streets, but in Kyoto it is the exception. Tokio also wears boots, but Kyoto is noisy with pattens night and day. Not only are there countless shops in Kyoto given up to porcelain, carvings, screens, bronzes, old armour, and so forth, but no matter how trumpery the normal stock in trade of the other shops, a number of them have a little glass case—a shop within a shop, as it were—in which a few rare and ancient articles of beauty are kept. A great deal of Japan is expressed in this pretty custom.

THE RICE FIELDS

My first experience of Japanese scenery of any wildness was gained while shooting the rapids of the Katsuragava, an exciting voyage among boulders in a shallow and often very turbulent stream in a steep and craggy valley a few miles from Kyoto. Previous to this expedition I had seen, from the train, only the trim rice fields,—each a tiny parallelogram with its irrigation channels as a boundary, so carefully tended that there is not a weed in the whole country. Japan is cut up into these absurd little squares, of which twenty and more would go into an ordinary English field. Often the terminal posts are painted a bright red; often a little row of family tombs is there too. The watermill is a common object of the country.

But birds are few and animals one sees never. Indeed in all my three weeks I saw no four-footed animals, except a dead rat, two pigs and one cat. I am excluding of course beasts of draught—horses and bullocks—which are everywhere. Not a cow, not a sheep, not a dog! but that there are cattle is proved by the proverbial excellence of Kobe steaks, which I tested and can swear to. In all my three weeks, both in cities and the country, I saw only one crying child. Of children there were millions, mostly boys, but only one was unhappy.

SURFACE MATERIALISM

In spite of Kyoto's eight hundred temples I could not get any but a materialistic concept of its inhabitants; and elsewhere this impression was emphasised. A stranger cannot, of course, know; he can but record his feelings, without claiming any authority for them. But I am sure I was never in a country where I perceived fewer indications of any spiritual life. Every one is busy; every one seems to be happy or at any rate not discontented; every one chatters and laughs and is, one feels, a fatalist. Sufficient unto the day! After all, it is the women of a nation that chiefly keep burning the sacred flame and pass it on; but in Japan, I understand, the women are far too busy in pleasing the men to have time for such duties; Japan is run by men for men. It is an unwritten law that a woman must never be anything but gay in her lord's presence, must never for a moment claim the privilege of peevishness.

As an instance of the Japanese woman's indifference to fate and readiness to oblige, I may say that we had on our ship two or three hundred girls in charge of a duenna or so, who were bound for Honolulu to be married to Japanese settlers there, to whom their photographs had been forwarded. These girls are known as "Picture Brides." At Honolulu their new proprietors awaited them, and I suppose identified and appropriated them, although to the European eye one face differed no whit from another.

The Japanese have the practical qualities that consort with materialism. They are quick to supply creature comforts; their hotels are well- managed; their cooks are excellent; their sign-posts are numerous and, I believe, very circumstantial; at the railway stations are lists of the show places in the neighbourhood; the telephone is general. But there are strange failings. The roads, for example, are often very bad, although so many motor-cars exist. Even in Tokio the puddles and mud are abominable. There is no fixed rule to force rickshaw men to carry bells. There is no rule of the road at all, so that the driver of a vehicle must be doubly alert, having to make up his mind not only as to what he is going to do himself, but also what the approaching driver is probably going to do. From time to time, I believe, a rule of the road has been tried, but it has always broken down.

The rickshaw bells are the more important, because the Japanese are not observant. They may see Fuji and stand for hours worshipping a spray of cherry blossom, but they do not see what is coming. Normally they look down.

The rickshaw is comfortable and speedy; but to be drawn about by a fellow-creature is a humiliating experience and I never ceased to feel too conspicuous and ashamed. I discovered also how easy it is to lose one's temper with these men. I used to sit and wonder if there had ever been a runaway, and I never hired a rickshaw without thinking of Mr. Anstey's story of the talking horse.

FIRST GLIMPSE OF FUJI

I left Kyoto for Yokohama on Wednesday night, March 17, 1920, at eleven, and Thursday, March 18, 1920, thus remains with me as a red-letter day, for it was then, at about half-past seven in the morning, that, lifting the blind of my sleeping compartment, I saw — almost within reach, as it seemed, dazzlingly white under its snow against a clear blue sky, with the sun flooding it with glory — Fujiyama. I was to see it again several times — for I went to Myanoshita for that purpose—but never again so startlingly and wonderfully as this.

When I am asked to name in a word the most beautiful thing I saw on my travels I mention Fujiyama instantly. There is nothing else to challenge it. Perhaps had I seen Everest from Darjeeling I might have a different story to tell; but I missed it. The Taj? Yes, the Taj is a divine work of man; but it has not the serene lofty isolation of this sublime mountain, rising from the plain alone and immense with almost perfect symmetry.

I was not to see Fujiyama again for a week or so, but in the meanwhile I saw the Daibutsu, the giant figure of Buddha, at Kamakura, in all its bland placidity. These were the only big things I found in Japan.

TWO FUNERALS

Yokohama is industrial and dirty everywhere but on the drive beside the harbour, and on the Bluff, where the rich foreigners live. I visited one house on this pleasant eminence and there was nothing in it to suggest that it was in Japan any more than in, say, Cheltenham. The form was English, the furniture was English, the pictures and books were English; photographs of school and college cricket elevens gave it the final home touch. Only in the garden were there exotic indications. The English certainly have the knack of carrying their atmosphere with them. I had noticed that often in India; but this Yokohama villa was the completest exemplification.

Wandering about the city I came one morning on a funeral procession that ought to have pleased Henry Ward Beecher, who, on the only occasion on which I heard him, when he was very old and I was very young, urged upon his hearers the importance of bright colours and flowers instead of the ordinary habiliments and accoutrements of woe. For when a soul is on its way to paradise, he said, we should be glad. The Yokohama cortege was headed by men bearing banners; then came girls all in white, riding in rickshaws; then the gaudy hearse; then priests in rickshaws; and finally the relations and friends. The effect conveyed was not one of melancholy; but even if every one had been in black, impressiveness would have been wanting, for no one can look dignified in a rickshaw.

Compared, however, with a funeral which I saw in Hong-Kong, the Yokohama ceremony was solemnity in essence. The Hong-Kong obsequies were those of a tobacco-magnate's wife and the widower had determined to spare no expense on their thoroughness. He had even offered, but without success, to compensate the tramway company for a suspension of the service, the result of his failure being that every few minutes the procession was held up to permit the cars to go by; which meant that instead of taking only two hours to pass any given point, it took three. The estimated cost of the funeral was one hundred thousand dollars and all Hong-Kong was there to see.

To Chinese eyes it doubtless had a sombre religious character, but to us it was merely a diverting spectacle of incredible prolongation. We were not wholly to blame in missing its sanctity, for the participants, who were more like mummers than mourners, had all been hired and were enjoying the day off. For the most part they merely wore their fancy dress and walked and talked or played instruments, but now and then there was a dragon and a champion boxing it and these certainly earned their money. At intervals came bearers with trays on which were comforts for the next world or symbolical devices, while, to infinity both in front and behind, banners and streamers and lanterns danced and jogged above all. A miracle-show of the middle ages can have been not unlike it.

THE LITTLE GEISHA

I left Japan, as I have said, just before the cherry-blossom festivities began, but I was able to see a number of the dances—which never change but are passed with exactitude, step for step, gesture for gesture and expression for expression, from one geisha to another—as performed by a child who was being educated for the profession. Although so young she knew accurately upwards of sixty dances, and the pick of these she executed for a few spectators, in a little fragile paper-walled house outside Yokohama, while her adoring aunt played the wistful repetitive accompaniments.

The little creature—a mere watch-chain ornament—had a typical Japanese face, half mask, half mischief, and a tiny high voice which now and then broke into the dance. But dances, strictly speaking, they are not. They are really posturing and the manoeuvres of a fan. To me they are strangely fascinating, and, with the music, almost more so than our Western ballets. But there is a difference between the ballet and the geisha dances, and it is so wide that there is no true comparison; for whereas the ballet stimulates and excites, these Japanese movements hypnotise and lull.

MANNERS

The public manners of the Japanese are not good. In all my solitary walks about Myanoshita I met with no single peasant who passed the time of day, and in the streets of Tokio English people were being jostled and stared at and treated without respect. It was a moment when Americans were unpopular, and the theory was broached that for fear of missing the chance to be rude to an American the Japanese became rude to all outlanders indiscriminately. One indeed gathered the impression that, except in Kyoto, which is a backwater, foreigners are no longer wanted. "Japan for the Japanese" would seem to be the motto: one day, not far distant, to be amended to "The World for Japan." I shall never forget the humiliation I suffered in a stockbroker's office in Tokio, into which, seeing the words "English spoken" over the door, I had ventured in the hope of being directed to an address I was seeking. Not a word of English did any one know, but the whole staff left its typewriters and desks to come and laugh. I was always willing to remove the gravity of Japanese children by my grotesque Occidentalism, but I have a very real objection to being a butt for the ridicule of grown-ups. Such an incident could not have occurred, I believe, anywhere else. But it is not only the foreigners to whom the Japanese are rude: they do nothing for their fellows either. The want of chivalry in trains and trams was conspicuous.

The ceremonial manners of the Japanese can, however, be more precise and formal than any I ever witnessed. A wedding reception chanced to be in progress in my Tokio hotel one afternoon, and through the open door I had glimpses of Japanese gentlemen in frock coats bowing to Japanese ladies and making perfect right angles as they did so. So elaborate indeed were the courtesies that to Western eyes they bordered dangerously on burlesque.

The destination that I was seeking when I entered the stock-broker's office was a certain book-store, and when I eventually found it I was asked a question by a Japanese youth that still perplexes me. It was in the English section, the principal volumes in which, as imported to supply Japanese demands, were American, and all bore either upon success in engineering and other professions and crafts, or on the rapid acquirement of wealth. "How to double your income in a week"; "How to get rich quickly"; "How to succeed in business"; and so forth; all preaching, in fact, the new gospel which is doing Japan no good. There were also, however, a certain number of novels, and one of the customers, a boy who looked as though he were still at school, noting my English appearance, brought a translation of Maupassant to me and asked me what "soul" meant—"A Woman's Soul" being the new title. Now I defy any one with no Japanese to make it clear to a Japanese boy with very little English what a woman's soul is.

THE PLAY

At Tokio I was present for an hour or so at a performance in a national theatre. It had been in progress for a long time when I entered and would continue long after I left, for that is the Japanese custom. In London people with too little to do are on occasion prepared to spend the whole day outside theatres waiting for the doors to open. They will then witness a two and a half hours' performance. But in Japan the plays go on from eleven a.m. to eleven p.m. and the audience bring their sustenance and tobacco with them. The seats are mats on the ground, and the actors reach the stage by a passage through the auditorium as well as from the wings. The scenery is very elementary, and there is always a gate which has to be opened when the characters pass through and closed after them, although it is isolated and has no contiguous wall or fence.

None of our Western morbid desire for novelty, I am told, troubles the Japanese play-goer, who is prepared to witness the same drama, usually based on an historical event or national legend thoroughly familiar to him, for ever and ever. It is as though the theatres in England were given up exclusively to, say, Shakespeare's Henry IV, V and VI sequence. On the occasion of my visit there was little of what we call acting, but endless elocution. During the performance the attendants walk about, with the persistence of constables during a London police-court hearing, carrying refreshments and little charcoal stoves. The signal for the next act is a deafening clicking noise made by one of the stage hands on two sticks, which gradually rises to a shattering crescendo as the curtain is drawn aside. It must be understood that the theatre that I am describing was set apart for national drama. In others there are topical farces and laughter is continuous; but I did not visit any. On board ship, however, we had a series of performances of such pieces by the Japanese cabin attendants and waiters, many of whom were professional actors. The Japanese passengers enjoyed them immensely.

MYANOSHITA

A whole week of my too short stay was given to Myanoshita, whither I was driven by the impossibility of retaining a room in either Yokohama or Tokio, and where I stayed willingly on, out of delight in the place itself. After being cooped up for so long on ships, and kept inactive under the heat of India, it was like a new existence to take immense walks among these mountains in the keen rarified air, even though there was both rain and snow. Myanoshita stands some four thousand feet high and is situated in a valley in which are many summer cottages and health resorts. The heart of this Alpine settlement is the Fujiya Hotel, where I was living, which is kept by an enterprising Americanised and European-ised Japanese proprietor and his very charming wife, Madame Ya-maguchi, whose father was the founder of the house, and, I believe, the discoverer of the district, and who herself is famous as a gra-cious hostess throughout Japan. No hotel so well or so thoughtfully administered have I ever stayed in; nor was I ever in another where the water for the bath gushes in from a natural hot spring. But hot springs are numerous in this region, while there is a gorge which I visited, some four miles distant, where boiling sulphur hisses and bubbles for ever and aye.

Many of the Myanoshita dishes were new to me and welcome. There is an excellent salad called "Slow," and the bamboo, which is Japan's best friend—serving the nation in scores of ways: as fences, as walls, as water-pipes, as supports, as carrying-poles, as thatch, as fishing- rods—here found its way into the salad bowl and was not distasteful. The custom of drinking a glass of orange juice before breakfast might well be adopted with us; but not the least of the oddities of England which I realised as I moved about the earth is our unwillingness to eat fruit. Japan also has a perfect mineral wa-ter, "Tansan."

When not making long expeditions to catch new glimpses of Fuji I roamed about the hill-sides among the little villages, or leaned over crazy bridges to watch the waterfalls beneath; for there is wa-ter everywhere, tumbling down to the distant ocean, a wedge of which can be seen from the hotel windows. This Japanese valley might be in Switzerland, save for the absence of any but human life. Not a cow, not a goat.

The labourers wear blue linen smocks, usually with some device upon them, and they merge into the landscape as naturally as French or Belgian peasants. These men, whether working on the soil or the roads, or engaged in cutting bamboos or building houses, wear the large straw hats that one sees in the old Japanese prints. Nothing has changed in their dress. But the modernized Japanese, the dweller in the cities or casual visitor to the country, pins his faith to the bowler. The bowler is so much his favourite headgear that he wears it often with native costume on his body. Perhaps it is to Japan that all the bowlers have gone, now that London has taken to the soft Homburg. It was odd to meet groups of these bizarre little men among the precipices: even stranger perhaps were their little ladies, especially on Sunday, in the gayest Japanese clothes, their faces plastered with rice powder and cigarettes in their mouths. Too many of them are disfigured by gold teeth, which are so common in Japan as to be almost the rule. An English resident assured me that I must not assume that the Japanese teeth are therefore unusually defective: often the gold is merely ostentation, a visible sign that the owner of the auriferous mouth is both alive to American progress and can afford it.

Even in Myanoshita Fujiyama has to be sought for and climbed for, the walls of rock that form the valley being so high and enclosing. But the result is worth every effort. Immediately above the hotel is a hill from whose summit the upper part of the enchanted mountain can be seen, and I ascended tortuously to this point within an hour of my arrival. The next day I walked to Lake Hakone (where the Emperor has a summer palace), some eight miles away, in the hope of getting Fuji's white crest reflected on its surface; but a veil of mist enshrouded all. And then twice I went to the edge of the watershed at the head of the valley: once struggling through the snow to the Otome Pass, on an immemorial and nearly perpendicular bridle path, and once by the modern road to the tunnel which, with characteristic address, the Japanese have bored through the rock, thus reducing a very steep gradient.

In the tunnel the icicles were hanging several feet long and as big as masts, and the air was biting. But one emerged suddenly upon a prospect the wonder of which probably cannot be excelled—a vast plain far below, made up of verdure and villages and lakes, with distant surrounding heights, and immediately in front, filling half the sky, Fuji himself. It is from this point, and from the ancient Otome Pass, a mile or so away on the same ridge, that the symmetry of the mountain is most perfect; and here one can best appreciate the simplicity of it, the quiet natural ease with which it rises above its neighbours. There was more snow on the slopes than when I had seen it from the train a few days before; and the sky again was without a cloud. I have never been so conscious of majestic serenity, without any concomitant feeling of awe. Fuji is both sublime and human.

No other country has a symbol like this. When the Japanese think of Japan they visualise Fuji: returning exiles crowd the decks for the first glimpse of it; departing exiles with tears in their eyes watch it disappear. There is not a shop window but has Fuji in some representation; it is found in every house; its contours are engraved on teaspoons, embossed on ash-trays. You cannot escape from its counterfeits; but if you have seen it you do not mind.

When on my way home I found myself in an American picture gallery, either in San Francisco, Chicago, Boston or New York, I lingered longest in the rooms where the coloured prints of the Japanese masters hang—and America has very fine collections, particularly in Boston—and I stood longest before those landscapes by Hokusai and Hiroshige in which Fuji occurs. Hokusai in particular venerated the mountain, and in many of his most beautiful pictures people are calling to each other to admire some new and marvellous aspect of it. It was he who drew Fuji as seen through the arch of a breaking wave! I was looking at the British Museum's example of this daring print only a few days ago, and, doing so, living my Myanoshita days again.

There is much in Japan that is petty, much that is too material and not a little that is disturbing; but Fuji is there too, dominating all, calm and wise and lovely beyond description, and it would be Fuji that lured me back.

AMERICA

DEMOCRACY AT HOME

My first experience of democracy-in-being followed swiftly upon boarding the steamboat for San Francisco, when "Show this man Number 231" was the American steward's command to a cabin boy. I had no objection to being called a man: far from it; but after years of being called a gentleman it was startling. This happened at Yokohama; and when, in the Customs House at San Francisco, a porter wheeling a truck broke through a queue of us waiting to obtain our quittances, with the careless warning, "Out of the way, fellers!" I knew that here was democracy indeed.

I confess to liking it, although I was to be brought up with another jolt when a notice-board on a grass-plot suddenly confronted me, bearing the words: —

[Illustration: KEEP OFF. THIS MEANS YOU.]

But I like it. I like the tradition which, once your name is written in the hotel reception book, makes you instantly "Mr. Lucas" to every one in the place. There is a friendliness about it: the hotel is more of a home, or at any rate, less of a barrack, because of it. And yet this universal camaraderie has some odd lapses into formality. The members of clubs in America are far more ceremonious with each other than we are in England. In English clubs the prefix "Mr." is a solecism, but in American clubs I have watched quite old friends and associates whose greetings have been marked almost by pomposity and certainly by ritual. Yet Americans, I should say, are heartier than we; more happy to be with each other; less critical and exacting. They certainly spend less time in discussing each other's foibles. That may be because the dollar is so much more an absorbing theme, but more likely it is because America is a democracy, and the theory of democracy, as I understand it, is to assume that every man is a good fellow until the reverse is proved. I should not like to say that the theory of those of us who live under a monarchy is the opposite, but it seemed to me that Americans are more ready than we to be sociable and tolerant.

Try as I might I could never be quick enough to get in first with that delightful American greeting, "Pleased to meet you," or "Glad to know you, Mr. Lucas." I pondered long on the best retort and at last formulated this, but never dared to use it for fear that its genuineness might be suspected: "I shall be sorry when we have to part."

SAN FRANCISCO

It was in San Francisco that I learned—and very quickly—that it is as necessary to visit America in order to know what Americans are like as it is to leave one's own country in order to know more about that. Americans when abroad are less hearty, less revealing. They are either suffering from a constraint or an over-assertiveness; and both moods may be due to not being at home. In neither case are they so natural as at home. I suppose that on soil not our own we all tend to be a little over-anxious to proclaim our nationality, to maintain the distinction. In our hats can perhaps be too firmly planted the invisible flag of our country.

Be this as it may, I very quickly discerned a difference between Americans in America and in England. I found them simple where I had thought of them as the reverse, and now, after meeting others in various parts of the country, even in complex and composite New York, I should say that simplicity is the keynote of the American character. It is in his simplicity that the American differs most from the European. Such simplicity is perfectly consistent with the impatience, the desire for novelty, for brevity, of the American people. We think of them as always wishing to reduce life to formulae, as unwilling to express any surprise, and these tendencies may easily be considered as signs of a tiring civilisation. But in reality they are signs of youth too.

ROADS GOOD AND BAD

San Francisco I shall chiefly recollect (apart from personal reasons) for the sparkling freshness and vigour of the air; for the extent and variety of Golden Gate Park, where I found a bust of Beethoven, but no sign of Bret Harte; for the vast reading-room in the library at Berkeley, a university which is so enchantingly situated, beneath such a sun, and in sight of such a bay, that I marvel that any work can be done there at all; and for the miles and miles of perfect tarmac roads fringed with burning eschscholtzias and gentle purple irises. That was in April. I found elsewhere in America no roads comparable with these. Even around Washington their condition was such that to ride in a motor- car was to experience all the alleged benefits of horseback, while in the Adirondacks, anywhere off the noble Theodore Roosevelt Memorial Highway, with its "T.R." blazonings along the route, one's liver was bent and broken. While I was in America the movement to purchase Roosevelt's house as a national possession was in full swing, but this Memorial Highway strikes the imagination with more force. That was an inspiration, and I hope that the road will never be allowed to fall into disrepair.

UNIVERSITIES, LOVE AND PRONUNCIATION

Watching the young men and maidens crowding to a lecture in the Hearst Amphitheatre at Berkeley, under that glorious Californian sky, I was struck by the sensible, frank intimacy of them all, and envied them the advantages that must be theirs over the English methods of segregation at the same age, which, by creating shyness and destroying familiarity, tends to retard if not destroy the natural understanding which ought to subsist between them and if it did would often make life afterwards so much simpler.

I asked one of the professors to what extent marriages were made in Berkeley, but he had no statistics. All he could say was that Cupid was very little trouble to the authorities and that Mr. Hoover and Mrs. Hoover first met each other as students at Stanford. And then I asked an ex-member of one of the Sororities and she said that at college one was a good deal in love and a good deal out of it. The romance rarely persisted into later life.

She pronounced romance with the accent on the first syllable, whereas somewhere half-way across the Atlantic the accent passes to the second; and why such illogical things should be is a mystery. The differences can be very disconcerting, especially if one refuses to give way. I had an experience to the point when talking with some one in Chicago and wishing to answer carefully his question as to the conditions under which the poor of our great cities live. These are, in my observation, infinitely worse in England than in America. Indeed I hardly saw any poor in America at all—not poverty as we understand it. But I could not frame my reply because "squalor" (which we pronounce as though it rhymed with "mollor") was the only fitting epithet and he had just used it himself, pronouncing it in the American way—or at any rate in his American way—with a long "a." So I turned the subject.

Neither nation has any monopoly of reasonableness in pronunciation. The American way of saying "advertisement" is more sensible than ours of saying "adver´tisment," since we say "advertise" too. But then, although the Americans say "inquire," just as we do, they illogically put the stress on the first syllable when they talk about an "in´quiry." The Tower of Babel is thus carried up one storey higher. The original idea was merely to confuse languages; it cannot ever have been wished that two friendly peoples should speak the same language differently.

But I have wandered far from Berkeley and Stanford. I am not sure as to my course of conduct if I had a daughter of seventeen, but I am quite convinced that if I had a son of that age I should send him to an American university for two or three years after his English school. He should then become a citizen of the Anglo-Saxon world indeed.

FIRST SIGNS OF PROHIBITION

We had met Prohibition first at Honolulu, not a few of the passengers receiving the shock of their lives on learning at the hotel that only "soft drinks" were permitted. Our second reminder of the new regime came as we entered American waters off the Golden Gate and the ship's bar was formally closed. And then, in San Francisco, we found "dry" land indeed. In this connection let me say that in the hotel I made acquaintance with an official of great power who was new to me: the buttoned boy who rejoices in the proud title of Bell Captain. He gave me a private insight into his precocity (but that is not the word, for all boys in America are men too), and into his influence, by offering to supply me with forbidden fruit, in the shape of whisky, at the modest figure of $25 a bottle. He did not, however, say dollars: like most of his compatriots (and it is a favourite word with them) he said something between "dollars" and "dallars."

I had, a few days later, in Chicago, a similarly friendly offer from a policeman of whom I had inquired the way. Recognizing an English accent, he had instantly divined what my dearest wish must be. I then asked him how prohibition was affecting the people on his beat. He said that a few drunkards were less comfortable and a few wives more serene; but for the most part he had seen no increase of happiness, and the extra money that it provided was spent either on the movies, dress, or "other foolishness." I did not allow him to refresh me. After a course of American "tough" fiction, of which "Susan Lenox" remains most luridly in the memory, I had a terror of all professional upholders of the law.

R.L.S.

Coming by chance upon the Robert Louis Stevenson memorial at San Francisco, on the edge of Chinatown, I copied its inscription, and in case any reader of these notes may have forgotten its trend I copy it again here; for I do not suppose that its application was intended to cease with the Californian city. It is counsel addressed to the individual, but since nations are but individuals in quantity such ideals cannot be repeated amiss:

To be honest; to be kind; to earn a little; to spend a little less; to make upon the whole a family happier for his presence; to renounce when that shall be necessary and not to be embittered; to keep a few friends, but these without capitulation; above all, on the same grim condition, to keep friends with himself—here is a task for all that man has of fortitude and delicacy.

It is a far cry from San Francisco to Saranac, yet Stevenson is their connecting chain, with the late Harry Widener's amazing collection of Stevensoniana, in his memorial library at Harvard, as a link. The Saranac cottage, which on the day of my visit was surrounded by the sweetest lilac blooms that ever perfumed the air, is still a place of pilgrimage, and one by one new articles of interest are being added to the collection. It was pleasant indeed to find an English author thus honoured. Later, in Central Park, New York, I was to find statues of Shakespeare, Burns and Sir Walter Scott.

It was, oddly enough, in the Adirondacks that I came upon my only experience of simplified spelling in the land of its birth. It was in that pleasant home from home, the Lake Placid Club, where one is adjured to close the door "tyt" as one leaves a room; where one drinks "cofi"; and where that most necessary and mysterious of the functionaries of life, the physician, is able to watch his divinity dwindle and his dignity disappear under the style "fizisn."

STORIES AND HUMOURISTS

I heard many stories in America, where every one is a raconteur, but none was better than this, which my San Francisco host narrated, from his own experience, as the most perfect example of an honest answer ever given. When a boy, he said, he was much in the company of an old trapper in the Californian mountains. During one of their expeditions together he noticed that a camp meeting was to be held, and out of curiosity he persuaded Reuben to attend it with him. Perched on a back seat, they were watching the scene when an elderly Evangelical sister placed herself beside the old hunter, laid her hand on his arm, and asked him if he loved Jesus. He pondered for some moments and then replied thus: "Waal, ma'am, I can't go so far as to say that I love Him. I can't go so far as that. But, by gosh, I'll say this—I ain't got nothin' agin Him."

The funniest spontaneous thing I heard said was the remark of a farmer in the Adirondacks in reply to my question, Had they recovered up there, from the recent war? "Yes," he said, they had; adding brightly, "Quite a war, wasn't it?"

In a manner of speaking all Americans are humourists. Just as all French people are wits by reason of the epigrammatic structure of their language, so are all Americans humourists by reason of the national stores of picturesque slang and analogy to which they have access. I think that this tendency to resort to a common stock instead of striving after individual exactitude and colour is to be deplored. It discourages thought where thought should be encouraged. Adults are, of course, beyond redemption, but parents might at least do something about it with their children. One of the cleverest American writers whom I met made no effort whatever to get beyond these accepted phrases as he narrated one racy incident after another. With the pen in his hand (or, more probably, the typewriter under his fingers) his sense of epithet is precise; but in his conversational stories men were as mad "as Sam Hill," injuries hurt "like hell," and a knapsack was as heavy "as the devil." We all laughed; but he should have had more of the artist's pride.

Three American professional humourists whom I had the good fortune to meet and be with for some time were Irvin Cobb, Don Marquis, and Oliver Herford, each authentic and each so different. Beneath Mr. Cobb's fun is a mass of ripe experience and sagacity. However playful he may be on the surface one is aware of an almost Johnsonian universality beneath. It would not be extravagant to call his humour the bloom on the fruit of the tree of knowledge (I am talking now only of the three as I found them in conversation). Don Marquis, while equally serious (and all the best humourists are serious at heart), has a more grotesque fancy and is more of a reformer, or, at any rate, a rebel. His dissatisfaction with hypocrisy provoked a scorn that Mr. Cobb is too elemental to entertain. Some day perhaps Don Marquis will induce an editor to print the exercises in unorthodoxy which he has been writing and which, in extract, he repeated to us with such unction; but I doubt it. They are too searching. But that so busy a man should turn aside from his work to dabble in religious satire seemed to me a very interesting thing; for nothing is so unprofitable — except to the honest soul of him who conceives it.

One of Don Marquis's more racy stories which I recollect is of a loafer in a country town who had the habit of dropping into the store every day at the time the free cheese was set on the counter, and buying very little in return. When the time came for the privilege to be withdrawn the loafer was outraged and aghast. Addressing the storekeeper (his friend for years) he summed up his ungenerosity in these terms: "Your soul, Henry," he said, "is so mean, that if there were a million souls like it in the belly of a flea, they'd be so far apart they couldn't hear each other holler."

As for Oliver Herford, he is an elf, a sprite, a creature of fantasy, who may be — and, I rejoice to say, is — in this world, but certainly is not of it. This Oliver is in the line of Puck and Mercutio and Lamb and Hood and other lovers and makers of nonsense, and it is we who ask for "more." He had just brought out his irresponsible but very searching exercise in cosmogony, "This Giddy Globe," dedicated to President Wilson ("with all his faults he quotes me still") and this was the first indigenous work I read on American soil. Oliver Herford is perhaps best known by his "Rubaiyat of a Persian Kitten," and there is a kitten also in "This Giddy Globe":

"Hurray!" cried the Kitten, "Hurray!"
  As he merrily set the sails,
"I sail o'er the ocean to-day
  To look at the Prince of Wales."

—this was when the Prince was making his triumphant visit to New York in 1919—

"But, Kitten," I said dismayed,
  "If you live through the angry gales
You know you will be afraid
  To look at the Prince of Wales."

Said the Kitten, "No such thing!
  Why should he make me wince?
If a Cat may look at a King
  A Kitten may look at a Prince!"

This reminds me that the story goes that when the Prince expressed his admiration for Fifth Avenue he was congratulated upon having "said a mouthful." Beyond a mouthful, as an encomium of sagacity or sensationalism in speech, there is but one advance and that is when one says "an earful."

THE CARS

The journey from San Francisco to Chicago, once the fruit country is passed, is drearily tedious, and I was never so tired of a train. The spacious compartments that one travelled in on the Indian journeys, where there are four arm-chairs and a bath-room, are a bad preparation for the long narrow American cars packed with humanity, and for the very inadequate washing-room, which is also the negro attendant's bed- chamber: "Although," he explained to me, "when the car isn't full I always sleep in Berth Number 1." If the night could be indefinitely prolonged, these journeys would be more tolerable; but for the general comfort the sleeping berths must be converted into seats at an early hour. In addition to books, I had, as a means of beguilement, the society of a returned exile from the Philippines, who told me the story of his life, showed me the necklace he was taking home to his daughter's wedding, and asked my advice as to the wisdom or unwisdom of marrying again, the lady of his wavering choice having been at school with him in New England and being now a widow in Nebraska with property of her own. Besides being thus garrulous and open, he was the most helpful man I ever met, acting as a nurse to the three or four restless children in the car, and even producing from his bag a pair of scissors and a bottle of gum with which to make dolls' paper clothes. Never in my life have I called a stranger "Ed" on such short acquaintance; never have I been called "Poppa" so often by the peevish progeny of others.

It was on this train that I began to realise how much thirstier the Americans are than we. The passengers were continually filling and emptying the little cups that are stacked beside the fountains in the corridors, and long before we reached Chicago the cups had all been used. In England only children drink water at odd times and they not to excess. But in America every one drinks water, and the water is there for drinking, pure and cold and plentiful. It is beside the bed, in the corners of offices, awaiting you at meals, jingling down the passages of hotels, bubbling in the streets. In English restaurants, water bottles are rarely supplied until asked for; in our hotel bedrooms they seldom bear lifting to the light. As to whether the general health of the Americans is superior or inferior to ours by reason of this water- drinking custom, I have no information; but figures would be interesting.

CHICAGO

In Chicago the weather was wet and cold, and it was not until after I had left that I learned of the presence there of certain literary collections which I may now perhaps never see. But I spent much time in the Museum, where there is one of the finest Hobbemas in the world, and where two such different creative artists as Claude Monet and Josiah Wedgwood are especially honoured. But the chief discovery for me was the sincere and masterly work in landscape of

George Inness, my first impression of whom was to be fortified when I passed on to Boston, and reinforced in the Hearn collection in the Metropolitan Museum in New York.

It was in Chicago, in the Marshall Field Book Department — which is to ordinary English bookshops like a liner to a houseboat — that I first realised how intense is the interest which America takes in foreign contemporary literature. In England the translation has a certain vogue — Mrs. Garnett's supple and faithful renderings of Turgenev, Tolstoi, Dostoievski, and Tchekov have, for example, a great following — but we do not adventure much beyond the French and the Russians; whereas I learn that English versions of hundreds of other foreign books are eagerly bought in America. Such curiosity seems to me to be very sensible. I was surprised also to find tables packed high with the modern drama. In England the printed play is not to the general taste.

It was in Chicago that I found "window-shopping" at its most enterprising. In San Francisco the costumiers' windows were thronged all Sunday, but in Chicago they are brilliantly lighted till midnight, long after closing hours, so that late passers-by may mark down desirable things to buy on the morrow.

The spirited equestrian statue of General John A. Logan, in a waste space by Michigan Avenue, which I could see from my bedroom window, was my first and by no means the least satisfying experience of American sculpture on its native soil — to be face to face with St. Gaudens' figure of "Grief" in Rock Creek Cemetery, at Washington, having long been a desire. In time I came to see that beautiful conception, and I saw also the fine Shaw monument in Boston, fine both in idea and in execution; and the Sheridan, by the Plaza Hotel in New York; and the Farragut in Madison Square; and the Pilgrim in Philadelphia — all the work of the same firm, sensitive hand, a replica of whose Lincoln is now to be seen at Westminster.

The statue seems almost as natural a part of civic ornament in America as it is in France, and is not in England; and the standard as a rule is high. In particular I like the many horsemen — Anthony Wayne dominating the landscape at Valley Forge; and George Washington again and again, and not least in Fairmount Park in Philadelphia (where there is also a bronze roughrider realistically set on a cliff—as though from Ambrose Bierce's famous story—by Frederic Remington). American painters can too often suggest predecessors, usually French, but the sculptors have a strength and directness of their own, and it would not surprise me if some of the best statues of the future came from their country. No one would say that all American civic sculpture is good. There is a gigantic bust of Washington Irving behind New York's Public Library which would be better away; nor are the lions that guard that splendid institution superabundantly leonine; but the traveller is more charmed than depressed by the marble and bronze effigies that meet his eye—and few witnesses have been able to say that of England. Among the more remarkable public works I might name the symbolical figures on the steps of the Boston Free Library, and the frieze in deep relief on the Romanesque church on Park Avenue in New York, and I found something big and impressive in the Barnard groups at Harrisburg. Many of the little bronzes in the Metropolitan Museum—at the other extreme—are exquisite.

THE MOVIES

We have our cinema theatres in England in some abundance, but the cinema is not yet in the blood here as in America. In America picture-palaces are palaces indeed—with gold and marble, and mural decorations, built to seat thousands—and every newspaper has its cinema page, where the activities of the movie stars in their courses are chronicled every morning. Moreover, America is the home of the industry; and rightly so, for it has, I should say, been abundantly proved that Americans are the only people who really understand both cinema acting and cinema production. Italy, France and England make a few pictures, but their efforts are half-hearted: not only because acting for the film is a new and separate art, but because atmospheric conditions are better in America than in Europe.

It was in Chicago that I had my only opportunity of seeing cinema stars in the flesh. The rain falling, as it seems to do there with no more effort or fatigue to itself than in Manchester, I had, one afternoon, to change my outdoor plans and take refuge at the matinee of a musical comedy called "Sometime," with Frank Tinney in the leading part. Tinney, I may say, during his engagement in London some years ago, became so great a favourite that one performer has been flourishing on an imitation of him ever since. The play had been in progress only for a few minutes when Frank, in his capacity as a theatre doorkeeper, was presented by his manager with a tip. A dialogue, which to the trained ear was obviously more or less an improvisation, then followed:

Manager: "What will you do with that dollar, Frank?"

Frank: "I shall go to the movies. I always go to the movies when there's a Norma Talmadge picture. Ask me why I always go to the movies when there's a Norma Talmadge picture."

Manager: "Why do you always go to the movies when there's a Norma Talmadge picture, Frank?"

Frank: "I go because, I go because she's my favourite actress. (*Applause*.) Ask me why Norma Talmadge is my favourite actress."

Manager: "Why is Norma Talmadge your favourite actress, Frank?"

Frank: "Norma Talmadge is my favourite actress because she is always saving her honour. I've seen her saving it seventeen times. (*To the audience*) You like Norma Talmadge, don't you?" (*Applause from the audience.*)

Frank: "Then wouldn't you like to see her as she really is? (*To a lady sitting with friends in a box.*) Stand up, Norma, and let the audience see you."

Here a slim lady with a tense, eager, pale face and a mass of hair stood up and bowed. Immense enthusiasm.

Frank: "That's Norma Talmadge. You do like saving your honour, don't you, Norma? And now (*to the audience*) wouldn't you like to see Norma's little sister, Constance? (*More applause.*) Stand up, Constance, and let the audience see you."

Here another slim lady bowed her acknowledgments and the play was permitted to proceed.

What America is going to do with the cinema remains to be seen, but I, for one, deplore the modern tendency of novelists to be lured by American money to write for it. If the cinema wants stories from novelists let it take them from the printed books. One has but to reflect upon what might have happened had the cinema been invented a hundred years ago, to realise my disturbance of mind. With Mr. Lasky's millions to tempt them Dickens would have written "David Copperfield" and Thackeray "Vanity Fair," not for their publishers and as an endowment to millions of grateful readers in perpetuity, but as plots for the immediate necessity of the film, with a transitory life of a few months in dark rooms. Of what new "David Copperfields" and "Vanity Fairs" the cinema is to rob us we shall not know; but I hold that the novelist who can write a living book is a traitor to his art and conscience if he prefers the easy money of the film. Readers are to be considered before the frequenters of Picture Palaces. His privilege is to beguile and amuse and refresh through the ages: not to snatch momentary triumphs and disappear.

The evidence of the moment is more on the side of the pessimist than the optimist. I found in America no trace of interest in such valuable records as the Kearton pictures of African jungle life or the Ponting records of the Arctic Zone. For the moment the whole energy of the gigantic cinema industry seemed to be directed towards the filming of human stories and the completest beguilement, without the faintest infusion of instruction or idealism, of the many-headed mob. In short, to provide "dope." Whether so much "dope" is desirable, is the question to be answered. That poor human nature needs a certain amount, is beyond doubt. But so much? And do we all need it, or at any rate deserve it? is another question. Sometimes indeed I wonder whether those of us who have our full share of senses ought to go to the cinema at all. It may be that its true purpose is to be the dramatist of the deaf.

THE AMERICAN FACE

Perhaps it is one of the travellers' illusions (and we are very susceptible to them), but I have the impression that American men are more alike than the English are. It may be because there are fewer idiosyncrasies in male attire, for in America every one wears the same kind of hat; but I think not. In spite of the mixed origin of most Americans, a national type of face has been evolved to which they seem satisfied almost universally to pay allegiance. Again and again in the streets I have been about to accost strangers to whom I felt sure I had recently been introduced, discovering just in time that they were merely doubles. In England I fancy there is more individuality in appearance. If it is denied that American faces are more true to one type than ours, I shall reopen the attack by affirming that American voices are beyond question alike. My position in these two charges may be illustrated by notices that I saw fixed to gates at the docks in San Francisco. On one were the words "No Smoking"; on the other "Positively No Smoking."

And what about the science of physiognomy? I have been wondering if Lavater is to be trusted outside Europe. In China and Japan I was continually perplexed, for I saw so many men who obviously were successful—leaders and controllers—but who were without more than the rudiments of a nose on which to support their glasses; and yet I have been brought up to believe that without a nose of some dimensions it was idle to hope for worldly eminence. Again, in America, is it possible that all these massive chins and firm aquiline beaks are ruling the roost and reaching whatever goal they set out for? I doubt it.

The average American face is, I think, keener than ours and healthier. One sees fewer ruined faces than in English cities, fewer men and women who have lost self-respect and self-control. The American people as a whole strike the observer as being more prosperous, more alert and ambitious, than the English. Where I found mean streets they were always in the occupation of aliens.

To revert to the matter of clothes, the American does as little as possible to make things easy for the conjectural observer. In England one can base guesses of some accuracy on attire. In a railway carriage one can hazard without any great risk of error the theory that this man is in trade and that in a profession, that another is a stockbroker, and a fourth a country squire. But America is full of surprises, due to the uniformity of clothing and a certain careless-ness which elevates comfort to a ritual. The man you think of as a millionaire may be a drummer, the drummer a millionaire. Again, in England people are known to a certain extent by the hotels they stay at, the restaurants they eat at, and the class in which they trav-el. Such superficial guides fail one in America.

PROHIBITION AGAIN

I can best indicate, without the mechanical assistance of dates, the time of my sojourn in New York by saying that, during those few weeks, Woodrow Wilson's successor was being sought, the possibil-ity of the repeal of the Prohibition Act was a matter of excited inter-est, and "Babe" Ruth was the national hero. During this period I saw the President sitting on the veranda of the White House; I had op-portunities of honouring Prohibition in the breach as well as in the observance; and these eyes were everlastingly cheered and enriched by the spectacle of the "Babe" (who is a baseball divinity) lifting a ball over the Polo Ground pavilion into Manhattan Field. I hold, then, that I cannot be said to have been unlucky or to have wasted my time.

I found (this was in the spring of 1920) Prohibition the universal topic: could it last, and should it last? In England we are accused of talking always of the weather. In America, where there is no weath-er, nothing but climate, that theme probably was never popular. Even if it once were, however, it had given way to Prohibition. At every lunch or dinner table at which I was present Prohibition was a topic. And how could it be otherwise?—for if my host was a "dry" man, he had to begin by apologising for having nothing cheering to offer, and if he possessed a cellar it was impossible not to open the ball by congratulating him on his luck and his generosity. Meanwhile the guests were comparing notes as to the best substitutes for alcoholic beverages, exchanging recipes, or describing their adventures with private stills.

I visited a young couple in a charming little cottage in one of the garden cities near New York, and found them equally divided in their solicitude over a baby on the top floor and a huge jar in the basement which needed constant skimming if the beer was to be worth drinking.

One effect of Prohibition which I was hoping for, if not actually expecting, failed to materialise. I had thought that the standard of what are called T.B.M. (Tired Business Men) theatrical shows might be higher if the tendency of alcohol to make audiences more tolerant (as it undoubtedly can do in London) were no longer operative. But these entertainments seemed, under teetotallers, no better.

THE BALL GAME

After seeing my first ball game or so I was inclined to suggest improvements; but now that I have attended more I am disposed to think that those in authority know more about it than I do, and that such blemishes as it appears to have are probably inevitable. For one thing, I thought that the outfield had too great an advantage. For another, not unassociated with that objection, I thought that the home-run hit was not sufficiently rewarded above the quite ordinary hit—"bunch-hit," is it?—that brings in a man or men. In the English game of "Rounders," the parent of baseball, a home-run hit either restores life to a man already out or provides the batting side with a life in reserve. To put a premium of this kind on so noble an achievement is surely not fantastic. So I thought. And yet I see now that the game must not be lengthened, or much of its character would go. It is its concentrated American fury that is its greatest charm. If a three-day cricket match were so packed with emotion we should all die of heart failure.

I thought, too, that it is illogical that a ground stroke behind the diamond should be a no-ball, and yet, should that ball be in the air and caught, the striker should be out. I thought it an odd example of lenience to allow the batsman as many strokes behind the catcher as he chanced to make. But the more baseball I see the more it enchants me as a spectacle, and these early questionings are forgotten.

Baseball and cricket cannot be compared, because they are as different as America and England; they can only be contrasted. Indeed, many of the differences between the peoples are reflected in the games; for cricket is leisurely and patient, whereas baseball is urgent and restless. Cricket can prosper without excitement, while excitement is baseball's life-blood, and so on: the catalogue could be indefinitely extended. But, though a comparison is futile, it may be interesting to note some of the divergences between the games. One of the chief is that baseball requires no specially prepared ground, whereas cricket demands turf in perfect order. Bad weather, again, is a more serious foe to the English than to the American game, for if the turf is soaked we cannot go on, and hence the number of drawn or unfinished matches in the course of a season. A two hours' game, such as baseball is, can, however, always be played off.

In baseball the pitcher's ball must reach the batter before it touches the ground; in cricket, if the ball did not touch the ground first and reach the batsman on the bound, no one would ever be out at all, for the other ball, the full-pitch as we call it, is, with a flat bat, too easy to hit, for our bowlers swerve very rarely: it is the contact with the ground which enables them to give the ball its extra spin or break. Full-pitches are therefore very uncommon. In cricket a bowler who delivered the ball with the action of a pitcher would be disqualified for "throwing": it is one of the laws of cricket that the bowler's elbow must not be bent.

In cricket (I mean in the first-class variety of the game) the decisions of the umpire are never questioned, either by players or public.

In baseball there are but two strokes for the batter: either the "swipe," or "slog," as we call it, where he uses all his might, or the "bunt," usually a sacrificial effort; in cricket there are scores of strokes, before the wicket, behind it, and at every angle to it. These the cricketer is able to make because the bat is flat and wide, and he holds it both vertically and at a slant, as occasion demands, and is allowed, at his own risk, to run out to meet the ball. In the early days of cricket, a hundred and fifty years ago, the bat was like a baseball club, but curved, and the only strokes then were much what the only baseball strokes are now—the full-strength hit and the stopping hit. So long as the pitcher delivers the ball in the air it is probable that the baseball club will remain as it is; but should the evolution of the game allow the pitcher to make use of the ground, then the introduction of a flattened club is probable. But let us not look ahead. All that we can be sure of is that, since baseball is American, it will change.

To resume the catalogue of contrast. In baseball the batsman must run for every fair hit; in cricket he may choose which hits to run for.

In baseball a man's desire is to hit the ball in the air beyond the fielders; in cricket, though a man would like to do this, his side is better served if he hits every ball along the ground.

In baseball no man can have more than a very small number of hits in a match; in cricket he can be batting for a whole day, and then again before the match is over. There are instances of batsmen making over 400 runs before being out.

Another difference between the games is that in cricket we use a new ball only at the beginning of a fresh inning (of which there cannot be more than four in a match) and when each 200 runs have been scored; and (this will astonish the American reader) when the ball is hit among the people it is returned. I have seen such rapid voluntary surrenders at baseball very seldom, and so much of a "fan" have I become that the spectacle has always been accompanied in my breast by pain and contempt. I had the gratification of receiving from the burly John McGraw an autograph ball as a souvenir of a visit to the Polo Ground. I put it in my pocket hurriedly, conscious of the risk I ran among a nation of ball- stealers in possessing such a trophy; and I got away with it. But I am sure that had it been a ball hit out of the ground by the mighty "Babe" Ruth, which—recovering it by some supernatural means—he had handed to me in public, I should not have emerged alive, or, if alive, not in the ball's company.

In cricket the wicket-keeper, who, like the baseball catcher, is protected, although he has no mask, is the most difficult man to obtain, because he has the hardest time and the least public approbation; in baseball the catcher is a hero and every boy aspires to his mitt.

In cricket no player makes more than three hundred pounds a season, unless it is his turn for his one and only benefit, when he may make a thousand pounds more. But most players do not reach such a level of success that a benefit is their lot. But baseballers earn enormous sums.

If a match could be arranged between eleven cricketers and eleven baseballers, the cricketers to be allowed to bowl and the baseballers to pitch, the cricketers to use their own bats and the baseballers their own clubs, I fancy that the cricketers would win; for the difficulty of hitting our bowling with a club would be greater than of hitting their pitching with a bat. But their wonderful fielding and far more accurate and swifter throwing than ours might just save them. Such throwing we see only very rarely, for good throwing is no longer insisted upon in cricket, much to the game's detriment. That old players should lose their shoulders is natural—and, of course, our players remain in first- class cricket for many years longer than ball champions—but there is no excuse for the young men who have taken advantage of a growing laxity in this matter. Chief of the few cricketers who throw with any of the terrible precision of a baseball field is Hobbs. It must be borne in mind, however, that cricket does not demand such constant throwing at full speed as baseball does; for in cricket, as I have said, the batsman may choose what hits he will run for, and if he chooses only the perfectly safe ones the fieldsmen are never at high pressure. There is also nothing in cricket quite to compare with base-stealing.

When it comes to catching, the percentage of missed catches is far higher at cricket than at baseball; but there are good reasons for this. One is that in baseball a glove is worn; another that in baseball all catches come to the fieldsmen with long or sufficient notice. The fieldsmen are all, except the catcher, in front of the batsmen; there is nothing to compare with the unexpected nimbleness that our point and slips have to display.

In the hypothetical contest that I have suggested, between baseballers and cricketers, if the conditions were nominally equal and the cricketers had to pitch like baseballers and the baseballers to use the English bat, why then the baseballers would win handsomely.

Baseball, I fancy, will not be acclimatised in England. We had our chance when London was full of American soldiers and we did not take it. But we were very grateful to them for playing the game in our midst, for the authorities were so considerate as to let them play on Sundays (which we are never allowed to do) and I was one of those who hoped that this might be the thin end of the wedge and Sunday cricket also be permitted. But no; when the war was over and the Americans left us, the old Sabbatarianism reasserted itself. If, however, we ever exchanged national games, and cricket were played in America and baseball in England, it is the English spectator who would have the better of the exchange. I am convinced that although we should quickly find baseball diverting, nothing would ever persuade an American crowd to be otherwise than bored by cricket.

SKYSCRAPERS

Perhaps if I had reached New York from the sea the skyscrapers would have struck me more violently. But I had already seen a few in San Francisco (and wondered at and admired the courage which could build so high after the earthquake of 1906), and more in Chicago, all ugly; so that when I came to New York and found that the latest architects were not only building high, but imposing beauty on these mammoth structures, surprise was mingled with delight. No matter how many more millions of dollars are expended on that strange medley of ancient forms which go to make up New York's new Cathedral, where Romanesque and Gothic seem already to be ready for their divorce, the Woolworth Building will be New York's true fane. Mr. Cass Gilbert, the designer of that graceful immensity, not only gave commerce its most notable monument (to date), but removed for ever the slur upon skyscrapers. The Woolworth Building does not scrape the sky; it greets it, salutes it with a *beau geste*. And I would say something similar of the Bush Building, with its alabaster chapel in the air which becomes translucent at night; and the Madison Square Tower (whose clock face, I noticed, has the amazing diameter of three storeys); and the Burroughs Welcome Building on 41st Street, with its lovely perpendicular lines; and that immense cube of masonry on Park Avenue which bursts into flower, so to speak, at the top in the shape of a very beautiful loggia. But even if these adornments become, as I hope, the rule, one could not resent the ordinary structural elephantiasis a moment after realising New York's physical conditions. A growing city built on a narrow peninsula is unable to expand laterally and must, therefore, soar. The problem was how to make it soar with dignity, and the problem has been solved.

In the old days when brown stone was the only builders' medium New York must have been a drab city indeed; or so I gather from the few ancient typical residences that remain. There are a few that are new, too, but for the most part the modern house is of white stone. Gayest of all is, I suppose, that vermilion-roofed florist's on Fifth Avenue.

One has to ascend the Woolworth Building to appreciate at a blow with what discretion the original settlers of New York made their choice. It is interesting, too, to watch Broadway — which, for all I know, is the longest street in the world — starting at one's feet on its lawless journey to Albany: lawless because it is almost the only sinuous thing in this city of parallelograms and has the effrontery to cross diagonally both Fifth Avenue and Sixth. Before leaving the Woolworth Building, I would say that there seemed to me something rather comically paradoxical in being charged 50 cents for access to the top of a structure which was erected to celebrate the triumph of a commercial genius whose boast it was to have made his fortune out of articles sold at a rate never higher than 10 cents.

Having dallied sufficiently on the summit — there are a trifle of fifty- eight floors, but an express lift makes nothing of them — I continued the implacable career of the tripper by watching for a while the deafening kerb market, which presented on that morning an odd appearance, more like Yarmouth beach than a financial centre, for there had been rain, and all the street operators were in sou'westers and sea-boots. There can be spasms of similar excitement in London, in the neighbourhood of Capel Court, but we have nothing that compares so closely with this crowd as Tattersall's Ring at Epsom just before the Derby.

A PLEA FOR THE AQUARIUM

It was a relief to resume my programme by entering that abode of the dumb and detached—the aquarium in Battery Park. For the kerb uproar "the uncommunicating muteness of fishes" was the only panacea. The Bronx Zoo is not, I think, except in the matter of buffalo and deer paddocks, so good as ours in London, but it has this shining advantage—it is free. So also is the Aquarium in Battery Park, and it was pleasing to see how crowded the place can be. In England all interest in living fish, except as creatures to be coaxed towards hooks and occasionally retained there, has vanished; on the site of old Westminster Aquarium the Wesleyans now manage their finances and determine their circuits, while the Brighton Aquarium, once famous all the world over, is a variety hall with barely a fin to its name.

After seeing the aquarium in Honolulu, which is like a pelagic rainbow factory, and the aquarium in New York with all its strange and beautiful denizens, I am a little ashamed of our English apathy. To maintain picture galleries, where, however beautiful and chromatic, all is dead, and be insensitive to the loveliness of fish, in hue, in shape and in movement, is not quite pardonable.

ENGLISH AND FRENCH INFLUENCES

In essentials America is American, but when it comes to inessentials, to trimmings, her dependence on old England was noticeable again and again as I walked about New York. The fashion which, at the moment, the print shops were fostering was for our racing, hunting and coaching coloured prints of a century ago, while in the gallery of the distinguished little Grolier Club I found an exhibition of the work of Randolph Caldecott and Kate Greenaway. In such old bookshops as I visited all the emphasis was—just then—laid upon Keats and Lamb and Shelley, whose first editions and presentation copies seem to be continually making the westward journey. I had not been in New York twenty-four hours before Keats' "Lamia," 1820—with an inscription from the author to Charles Lamb—the very copy from which, I imagine, Lamb wrote his review, was in my hands; but it would have been far beyond my means even if the pound were not standing at 3.83. These "association" books, in which American collectors take especial pleasure, can be very costly. At a sale soon after I left New York, seven presentation copies of Dickens' books, containing merely the author's signed inscription, realised 4870 dollars. To continue, in Wanamaker's old curiosity department I found little but English furniture and odds and ends, at prices which in their own country would have been fantastically high. In the "Vanity Fair" department, however (as I think it is called), the source was French. I suppose that French influence must be at the back of all the costumiers and jewellers of New York, but the shops themselves are far more spacious than those in Paris and not less well-appointed. Tiffany's is a palace; all it lacks is a name, but its splendid anonymity is, I take it, a point of honour.

It used to be said that good Americans when they died went to Paris. The Parisian lure no doubt is still powerful; but every day I should guess that more of Paris comes to America. The upper parts of New York have boulevards and apartment houses very like the real thing, and I noticed that the architecture of France exerts a special attraction for the rich man decreeing himself a pleasure dome. There are millionaires' residences in New York that might have been transplanted not only from the Avenue du Bois de Boulogne, but from Touraine itself; while when I made my pilgrimage to Mr. Widener's, just outside Philadelphia, I found Rembrandt's "Mill," and Manet's dead bull-fighter, and a Vermeer, and a little meadow painted divinely by Corot, and El Greco's family group, and Donatello's St. George, and one of the most lovely scenes that ever was created by Turner's enchanted brush, all enshrined in a palace which Louis Seize might have built.

But America is even more French than this. Her women can be not less *soignées* than those of France, although they suggest a cooler blood and less dependence on male society; her bread and coffee are better than France's best. Moreover, when it comes to night and the Broadway constellations challenge the darkness, New York leaves Paris far behind. For every cabaret and supper resort that Paris can provide, New York has three; and for every dancing floor in Paris, New York has thirty. Good Americans, however, will still remain faithful to their old posthumous love, if only for her wine.

Apropos of American women, their position struck me as very different from the position of women with us. English women are deferential to their husbands; they are content to be relegated to the background on all occasions when they are not wanted. They are dependent. They seldom wear an air of triumph and rarely take the lead. But American women are complacent and assured, they do most of the talking, make most of the plans: if they are not seen, it is because they are in the background; they are either active prominently elsewhere or are high on pedestals. With each other they are mostly or often humorously direct, whereas with men they seem to adopt an ironical or patronising attitude. American women seem also to have a curious power of attracting to themselves other women who admire them and foster their self-esteem. And, for all that I know, these satellites have satellites too. Their federacy almost amounts to a solid secret society; not so much against men, for men must provide the sinews of war and other comforts, but for their own satisfaction. Both sexes appear not to languish when alone.

SKY-SIGNS AND CONEY ISLAND

All visitors to New York speak of the exhilaration of its air, and I can but repeat their testimony. After the first few days the idea of going to bed became an absurdity.

Among the peculiarly beautiful effects that America produces, sky signs must be counted high. I had seen some when in San Francisco against the deep Californian night, and they captivated the startled vision; but the reckless profusion and movement of the Great White Way, as I turned out of 42nd Street on my first evening in New York, came as something more than a surprise: a revelation of wilful gaiety. We have normally nothing in England to compare with it. Nor can we have even our Earl's Court exhibition imitations of it so long as coal is so rare and costly. But though we had the driving power for the electricity we could never get such brilliance, for the clear American atmosphere is an essential ally. In our humid airs all the diamond glints would be blurred.

For the purest beauty of traceries of light against a blue background one must go, however, not to Broadway, which is too bizarre, but to Luna Park on Coney Island. Odd that it should be there, in that bewildering medley of sound and restlessness, that an extreme of loveliness should be found; but I maintain that it is so, that nothing more strangely and voluptuously beautiful could be seen than all those minarets and domes, with their lines and curves formed by myriad lamps, turning by contrast the heavens into an ocean of velvet blue, mysterious and soft and profound.

Only periodically—when we have exhibitions at Earl's Court or at Olympia—is there in England anything like Coney Island. At Blackpool in August, and on Hampstead Heath on Bank Holidays, a corresponding spirit of revelry is attempted, but it is not so natural, and is vitiated by a self-conscious determination to be gay and by not a little vulgarity. The revellers of Steeplechase Park seemed to me to be more genuine even than the crowds that throng the Fête de Neuilly; and a vast deal happier.

One very striking difference between Coney Island and the French fair is the absence of children from New York's "safety-valve," as some one described it to me. I saw hardly any. It is as though once again the child's birthday gifts had been appropriated by its elders; but as a matter of fact the Parks of Steeplechase and Luna were, I imagine, designed deliberately for adults. Judging by the popularity of the chutes and the whips, the switchbacks and the witching waves, eccentric movement has a peculiar attraction for the American holiday-maker. As some one put it, there is no better way, or at any rate no more thorough way, of throwing young people together. Middle-aged people, too. But the observer receives no impression of moral disorder. High spirits are the rule, and impropriety is the exception. Even in the auditorium at Steeplechase Park, where the *cognoscenti* assemble to witness the discomfiture of the uninitiated, there is nothing but harmless laughter as the skirts fly up before the unsuspected blast. Such a performance in England, were it permitted, would degenerate into ugliness; in France, too, it would make the alien spectator uncomfortable. But the essential public chastity of the Americans—I am not sure that I ought not here to write civilisation of the Americans—emerges triumphant.

It was at Coney Island that I came suddenly upon the Pig Slide and had a new conception of what quadrupeds can do for man.

The Pig Slide, which was in one of the less noisy quarters of Luna Park, consisted of an enclosure in which stood a wooden building of two storeys, some five yards wide and three high. On the upper storey was a row of six or eight cages, in each of which dwelt a little live pig, an infant of a few weeks. In the middle of the row, descending to the ground, was an inclined board, with raised edges, such as is often installed in swimming-baths to make diving automatic, and beneath each cage was a hole a foot in diameter. The spectators and participants crowded outside the enclosure, and the thing was to throw balls, which were hired for the purpose, into the holes. Nothing could exceed the alert and eager interest taken by the little pigs in the efforts of the ball-throwers. They quivered on their little legs; they pressed their little noses against the bars of the cages; their little eyes sparkled; their tails (the only public cork-screws left in America) curled and uncurled and curled again: and with reason, for whereas if you missed— as was only too easy— nothing happened: if you threw accurately the fun began, and the fun was also theirs.

This is what occurred. First a bell rang and then a spring released the door of the cage immediately over the hole which your ball had entered, so that it swung open. The little pig within, after watching the previous infirmity of your aim with dejection, if not contempt, had pricked up his ears on the sound of the bell, and now smiled a gratified smile, irresistible in infectiousness, and trotted out, and, with the smile dissolving into an expression of absolute beatitude, slid voluptuously down the plank: to be gathered in at the foot by an attendant and returned to its cage all ready for another such adventure.

It was for these moments and their concomitant changes of countenance that you paid your money. To taste the triumph of good marksmanship was only a fraction of your joy; the greater part of it consisted in liberating a little prisoner and setting in motion so much ecstasy.

THE PRESS

America is a land of newspapers, and the newspapers are very largely the same. To a certain extent many of them are exactly the same, for the vastness of the country makes it possible to syndicalise various features, so that you find Walt Mason's sagacious and merry and punctual verse, printed to look like prose but never disappointing the ear, in one of the journals that you buy wherever you are, in San Francisco, Salt Lake City, Chicago or New York; and Mr. Montagu's topical rhymes in another; and the daily adventures of Mutt and Jeff, who are national heroes, in a third. Every day, for ever, do those and other regular features occur in certain of the papers: which is partly why no American ever seems to confine himself, as is our custom, to only one.

Another and admirable feature of certain American papers is a column edited by a man of letters, whose business it is to fill it every day, either with the blossoms of his own intelligence or of outside contributors, or a little of each: such a column as Don Marquis edits for *The Sun*, called "The Sundial," and Franklin R. Adams for *The Tribune*, called "The Conning Tower," and Christopher Morley for the New York *Evening Post*, called "The Bowling Green." Perhaps the unsigned "Way of the World" in our *Morning Post* is the nearest London correlative.

These columns are managed with skill and catholicity, and they impart an element of graciousness and fancy into what might otherwise be too materialistic a budget. A journalist, like myself, is naturally delighted to find editors and a vast public so true to their writing friends. Very few English editors allow their subscribers the opportunity of establishing such steady personal relations; and in England, in consequence, the signed daily contribution from one literary hand is very rare—to an American observer probably mysteriously so. The daily cartoon is common with us; but in London, for example, I cannot think of any similar literary feature that is signed in full. We have C.E.B.'s regular verse in the *Evening News* and "The Londoner's" daily essay in the same paper, and various initials elsewhere; but, with us, only the artists are allowed their names. Now, in America every name, everywhere, is blazoned forth.

Whatever bushel measures may be used for in the United States the concealing of light is no part of their programme.

Another feature of American daily journals comparatively unknown in England is the so-called comic pictorial sequence. All the big papers have from one to half a dozen of these sequences, each by a different artist. Bud Fisher with "Mutt and Jeff" comes first in popularity, I believe, and then there are his rivals and his imitators. Nothing more inane than some of these series could be invented; and yet they persist and could not, I am told, be dropped by any editor who thought first of circulation.

After the individual contributions have been subtracted, all the newspapers are curiously alike. The same reporters might be on every one; the same sub-editors; the same composers of head-lines. If we think of Americans as too capable of cynical levity it is largely because of these head-lines, which are always as epigrammatic as possible, always light-hearted, often facetious, and often cruel. An unfortunate woman's failure at suicide after killing her husband was thus touched off in one of the journals while I was in New York:

POOR SHOT AT HERSELF BUT SUCCEEDS IN LODGING BULLET IN SPOUSE.

When it comes to the choice of news, one cannot believe that American editors are the best friends of their country. I am holding no brief for many English editors; I think that our papers can be common too, and can be too ready to take things by the wrong handle; but I think that more vulgarising of life is, at present, effected by American journalists than by English. There are, however, many signs that we may catch up.

Profusion is a characteristic of the American newspaper. There is too much of everything. And when Sunday comes with its masses of reading matter proper to the Day of Rest one is appalled. One thing is certain— no American can find time to do justice both to his Sunday paper and his Maker. It is principally on Sunday that one realises that if Matthew Arnold's saying that every nation has the newspapers it deserves is true, America must have been very naughty. How the Sunday editions could be brought out while the paper-shortage was being discussed everywhere, as it was during my visit, was a problem that staggered me. But that the shortage was real I was assured, and jokes upon it even got into the music halls: a sure indication of its existence. "If the scarcity of paper gets more acute," I heard a comedian say, "they'll soon have to make shoes of leather again."

But it is not only the Sunday papers that are so immense. I used to hold the *Saturday Evening Post* in my hands, weighed down beneath its bulk, and marvel that the nation that had time to read it could have time for anything else. The matter is of the best, but what would the prudent, wise and hard-working philosopher who founded it so many years ago—Benjamin Franklin—say if he saw its lure deflecting millions of readers from the real business of life?

When we come to consider the American magazines—to which class the *Saturday Evening Post* almost belongs—and the English, there is no comparison. The best American magazines are wonderful in their quality and range, and we have nothing to set beside them. It is astonishing to think how different, in the same country, daily and monthly journalism can be. Omitting the monthly reviews, *Blackwood* is, I take it, our finest monthly miscellany; and all of *Blackwood* could easily and naturally be absorbed in one of the American magazines and be illustrated into the bargain, and still leave room for much more. And the whole would cost less! Why England is so poorly and pettily served in the matter of monthly magazines is something of a mystery; but part of the cause is the rivalry of the papers, and part the smallness of our population. But I shall always hold that we deserve more good magazines than we have now.

TREASURES OF ART

I was fortunate in being in New York when the Metropolitan Museum celebrated the fiftieth anniversary of its birth, for I was therefore able to enjoy not only its normal treasures but such others as had been borrowed for birthday presents, which means that I saw Mrs. H. E. Huntington's Vermeer, as well as the supreme Marquand example of that master; more than the regular wealth of Rembrandts, Manet's "Still Life," Gauguin's "Women by the River," El Greco's "View of Toledo," Franz Hals' big jovial Dutchman from Mr. Harry Goldman's walls, and Bellini's "Bacchanale"—to say nothing of the lace in galleries 18 and 19, Mr. Morgan's bronze Eros from Pompeii, and the various cases of porcelain from a score of collections. But without extra allurements I should have been drawn again and again to this magnificent museum.

Two of the principal metropolitan donors—Altman and Hearn—were the owners of big dry goods stores, while Marquand, whose little Vermeer is probably the loveliest thing in America, was also a merchant. In future I shall look upon all the great emporium proprietors as worthy of patronage, on the chance of their being also beneficent collectors of works of art. This thought, this hope, is more likely to get me into a certain Oxford Street establishment than all the rhetoric and special pleading of Callisthenes.

The Frick Gallery was not accessible; but I was privileged to roam at will both in Mr. Morgan's library and in Mr. H. E. Huntington's, in each of which I saw such a profusion of unique and unappraisable autographs as I had not supposed existed in private hands. Rare books any one with money can have, for they are mostly in duplicate; but autographs and "association" books are unique, and America is the place for them. I had known that it was necessary to cross the Atlantic in order to see the originals of many of the pictures of which we in London have only the photographs. I knew that the bulk of the Lamb correspondence was in America, and at Mr. Morgan's I saw the author's draft of the essay on "Roast Pig," and at Mr. Newton's, in Philadelphia, the original of "Dream Children," an even more desirable possession; I knew that America had provided an eager home for everything connected with Keats and Shelley and Stevenson; but it was a surprise to find at Mr. Morgan's so wide a range of MSS., extending from Milton to Du Maurier, and from Bacon to "Dorian Gray"; while at Mr. Huntington's I had in my hands the actual foolscap sheets on which Heine composed his "Florentine Nights."

I ought, you say, to have known this before. Maybe. But that ignorance in such matters is no monopoly of mine I can prove by remarking that many an American collector with whom I have talked was unaware that the library of Harvard University is the possessor of all the works of reference—mostly annotated—which were used by Thomas Carlyle in writing his "Cromwell" and his "Frederick the Great," and they were bequeathed by him in his will to Harvard University because of his esteem and regard for the American people, "particularly the more silent part of them."

My hours in these libraries, together with a glimpse of the Widener room at Harvard and certain booksellers' shelves, gave me some idea of what American collectors have done towards making the New World a treasury of the Old, and I realised how more and more necessary it will be, in the future, for all critics of art in whatever branch, and of literature in whatever branch, and all students even of antiquity, if they intend to be thorough, to visit America. This I had guessed at, but never before had known.

The English traveller lighting upon so many of the essentially English riches as are conserved in American libraries, and particularly when he has not a meagre share of national pride, cannot but pause to wonder how it came about—and comes about—that so much that ought to be in its own country has been permitted to stray.

In England collectors and connoisseurs are by no means rare. What, then, were they doing to let all these letters of Keats and Shelley, Burns and Byron, Lamb and Johnson—to name for the moment nothing else—find their resting-place in America? The dollar is very powerful, I know, but should it have been as pre-eminently powerful as this? Need it have defeated so much patriotism?

Pictures come into a different category, for every artist painted more than one picture. I have experienced no shade of resentment towards their new owners in looking at the superb collections of old and new foreign masters in the American public and private galleries; for so long as there are enough examples of the masters to go round, every nation should have a share. With MSS., however, it is different. Facsimiles, such as the Boston Bibliographical Society's edition of Lamb's letters, would serve for the rest of the world, and the originals should be in their author's native land. But that is a counsel of perfection. The only thing to do is to grin and bear it, and feel happy that these unique possessions are preserved with such loving pride and care. Any idea of retaliation on America on the part of England by buying up the MSS. of the great American writers, such as Franklin and Poe, Hawthorne and Emerson, Thoreau and Lowell, Holmes and Whitman, was rendered futile by the discovery that Mr. Morgan possesses these too. I had in his library all the Breakfast Table series in my hands, together with a play by Poe not yet published.

MOUNT VERNON

Mention of the beautiful solicitude with which these treasures are surrounded, suggests the reflection that the old country has something to learn from the new in the matter of distinguished custodianship. We have no place of national pilgrimage in England that is so perfect a model as Washington's home at Mount Vernon. It is perhaps through lack of a figure of the Washington type that we have nothing to compare with it; for any parallel one must rather go to Fontainebleau; but certain shrines are ours and none of them discloses quite such pious thoroughness as this. When I think of the completeness of the preservation and reconstruction of Mount Vernon, where, largely through the piety of individuals, a thousand personal relics have been reassembled, so that, save for the sightseers, this serene and simple Virginian mansion is almost exactly as it was, I am filled with admiration. For a young people largely in a hurry to find time to be so proud and so reverent is a significant thing.

Nor is this spirit of pious reverence confined to national memorials. Longfellow's Wayside Inn in Massachusetts, although still only a hostelry, compares not unfavourably with Dove Cottage at Grasmere and Carlyle's house in Chelsea. The preservation is more minute. But to return to Mount Vernon, the orderliness of the place is not its least noticeable feature. There is no mingling of trade with sentiment, as at Stratford-on-Avon, for example. Within the borders of the estate everything is quiet. I have never seen Americans in church (not, I hasten to add, because they abstain, but because I did), but I am sure that they could not, even there, behave more as if the environment were sacred. To watch the crowds at Mount Vernon, and to contemplate the massive isolated grandeur of the Lincoln Memorial now being finished at Washington, is to realise that America, for all its superficial frivolity and cynicism, is capable of a very deep seriousness.

VERS LIBRE

It would have been pedantic, while in America, to have abstained from an effort at *vers libre*.

REVOLT

I had been to the Metropolitan Museum looking at beautiful things and rejoicing in them.

And then I had to catch a train and go far into the country, to Paul Smith's.

And as the light lessened and the brooding hour set in I looked out of the window and reconstructed some of the lovely things I had seen — the sculptures and the paintings, the jewels and the porcelain: all the fine flower of the arts through the ages.

It seemed marvellous beyond understanding that such perfection could exist, and I thought how wonderful it must be to be God and see His creatures rising now and again to such heights.

And then I came to a station where there was to be a very long wait, and
I went to an inn for a meal.

It was a dirty neglected place, with a sullen unwashed man at the door, who called raspingly to his wife within.

And when she came she was a slattern, with dishevelled hair and a soiled dress and apron, and she looked miserable and worn out.

She prepared a meal which I could not eat, and when I went to pay for it I found her sitting dejectedly in a chair looking with a kind of dumb despair at the day's washing-up still to do.

And as I walked up and down the road waiting for the car I thought of this woman's earlier life when she was happy.

I thought of her in her courtship, when her husband loved her and they looked forward to marriage and he was tender and she was blithe.

They probably went to Coney Island together and laughed with the rest.

And it seemed iniquitous that such changes should come about and that merry girls should grow into sluts and slovens, and ardent young husbands should degenerate into unkempt bullies, and houses meant for happiness should decay, and marriage promises all be forgotten.

And I felt that if the world could not be better managed than that I never wanted to see any of God's artistic darlings at the top of their form again and the Metropolitan Museum could go hang.

DOMESTIC ARCHITECTURE

I believe that few statements about America would so surprise English people as that it has beautiful architecture. I was prepared to find Boston and Cambridge old-fashioned and homelike—Oliver Wendell Holmes had initiated me; I had a distinct notion of the cool spaciousness of the White House and the imposing proportions of the Capitol and, of course, I knew that one had but to see the sky-scrapers of New York to experience the traditional repulsion! But of the church of St. Thomas on Fifth Avenue I had heard nothing, nor of Mr. Morgan's exquisite library, nor of the Grand Central termi-nus, nor of the Lincoln Memorial at Washington, nor of the bland charm of Mount Vernon. Nor had I expected to find Fifth Avenue so dignified and cordial a thoroughfare.

Even less was I prepared for such metal work and stone work as is to be seen in some of the business houses—such as, for example, the new Guaranty Trust offices, both on Broadway and in Fifth

Avenue. Even the elevators (for which we in England, in spite of our ancient lethargy, have a one-syllable word) are often finished with charming taste.

Least of all did I anticipate the maturity of America's buildings. Those serene façades on Beacon Street overlooking Boston Common, where the Autocrat used to walk (and I made an endeavour to follow his identical footsteps, for he was my first real author)—they are as satisfying as anything in Georgian London. And I shall long treasure the memory of the warm red brick and easy proportions of the Boston City Hall and Faneuil Hall, and Independence Hall at Philadelphia seen through a screen of leaves. But in England (and these buildings were English once) we still have many old red brick buildings; what we have not is anything to correspond with the spacious friendly houses of wood which I saw in the country all about Boston and at Cambridge—such houses as that which was Lowell's home—each amid its own greenery. Nowhere, however, did I see a more comely manor house of the old Colonial style than Anthony Wayne's, near Daylesford, in Pennsylvania. In England only cottages are built of wood, and I rather think that there are now by-laws against that.

Not all the good country houses, big and little, are, however, old. American architects in the past few years seem to have developed a very attractive type of home, often only a cottage, and I saw a great number of these on the slopes of the Hudson, all the new ones combining taste with the suggestion of comfort. The conservation of trees wherever possible is an admirable feature of modern suburban planning in America. In England the new suburb too often has nothing but saplings. In America, again, the houses, even the very small ones, are more often detached than with us.

BOSTON

Once the lay-out of New York has been mastered—its avenues and numbered cross streets—it is the most difficult city in the world in which to lose one's way. But Boston is different. I found Boston hard to learn, although it was a pleasant task to acquire knowledge, for I was led into some of the quietest little Georgian streets I have ever been in, steep though some of them were, and along one of the fairest of green walks— that between the back of Beacon Street and the placid Charles.

Against Boston I have a certain grudge, for I could find no one to direct me to the place where the tea was thrown overboard. But that it was subjected to this indignity we may be certain—partly from the testimony of subsequent events not too soothing to English feelings, and partly from the unpopularity which that honest herb still suffers on American soil. Coffee, yes; coffee at all times; but no one will take any but the most perfunctory interest in the preparation of tea. I found the harbour; I traversed wharf after wharf; but found no visible record of the most momentous act of jettison since Jonah. In the top room, however, of Faneuil Hall, in the Honourable Artillery Company's headquarters, the more salient incidents of the struggle which followed are all depicted by enthusiastic, if not too talented, painters; and I saw in the distance the monument on Bunker's Hill.

My cicerone must be excused, for he was a Boston man, born and bred, and I ought never to have put him to the humiliation of confessing his natural ignorance. But the record is there, and legible enough. The tablet (many kind correspondents have informed me since certain of these notes appeared in the *Outlook*) is at 495 Atlantic Avenue, in the water-front district, just a short walk from the South Station, and it has the following inscription:

* * * * *

HERE FORMERLY STOOD

GRIFFIN'S WHARF

at which lay moored on Dec. 16, 1773, three British ships with cargoes of tea. To defeat King George's trivial but tyrannical tax of three pence a pound, about ninety citizens of Boston, partly disguised as Indians, boarded the ships, threw the cargoes, three hundred and forty- two chests in all, into the sea and made the world ring with the patriotic exploit of the

BOSTON TEA PARTY

"No! ne'er was mingled such a draught
  In palace, hall, or arbor,
 As freemen brewed and tyrants quaffed
  That night in Boston Harbor."

* * * * *

Boston has a remarkable art gallery and museum, notable for its ancient Chinese paintings, its collection of Japanese prints—one of the best in the world, I believe—and a dazzling wall of water-colours by Mr. Sargent. It was here that I saw my first Winslow Homers—two or three rapid sketches of fishermen in full excite-ment—and was conquered by his verve and actuality. In the Metro-politan Museum in New York I found him again in oils and my admiration increased. Surely no one ever can have painted the sea with more vividness, power and truth! We have no example of his work in any public gallery in London; nor have we anything by W. M. Chase, Arthur B. Davies, Swain Gifford, J. W. Alexander, George Inness, or De Forest Brush. It is more than time for another Ameri-can Exhibition. As it is, the only modern American artists of whom there is any general knowledge in England are Mr. Sargent, Mr. Epstein and Mr. Pennell, and the late E. A. Abbey, G. H. Boughton, and Whistler. Other Americans painting in our midst are Mr. Mark Fisher, R.A., Mr. J. J. Shannon, R.A., Mr. J. McLure Hamilton, and Mr. G. Wetherbee.

The Boston Gallery is the proud possessor of the rough and unfin-ished but "speaking" likeness of George Washington by his predes-tined limner Gilbert Stuart, and also a companion presentment of Washington's wife. Looking upon this lady's countenance and watching a party of school girls who were making the tour of the rooms, not uncomforted on their arduous adventure by chocolate and other confections, it occurred to me that if America increases her present love of eating sweets, due, I am told, not a little to Pro-hibition, George Washington will gradually disappear into the background and Martha Washington, who has already given her name to a very popular brand of candy, will be venerated instead, as the Sweet Mother of her Country.

An American correspondent sends me the following poem in order to explain to me the deviousness of Boston's principal thoroughfare. The poet is Mr. Sam Walter Foss: —

One day through the primeval wood
A calf walked home, as good calves should;

But made a trail all bent askew,
A crooked trail, as all calves do.

Since then two hundred years have fled,
And, I infer, the calf is dead.

But still he left behind his trail,
And thereby hangs my moral tale.

The trail was taken up next day
By a lone dog that passed that way;

And then a wise bell-wether sheep
Pursued the trail o'er vale and steep,

And drew the flock behind him too,
As good bell-wethers always do.

And from that day o'er hill and glade
Through those old woods a path was made,

And many men wound in and out,
And dodged and turned and bent about,

And uttered words of righteous wrath
Because 'twas such a crooked path;

But still they followed—do not laugh—
The first migrations of that calf,

And through this winding wood-way stalked
Because he wabbled when he walked.

The forest path became a lane
That bent and turned and turned again;

This crooked lane became a road,
Where many a poor horse with his load

Toiled on beneath the burning sun,
And travelled some three miles in one.

And thus a century and a half
They trod the footsteps of that calf.

The years passed on in swiftness fleet,
The road became a village street,

And then before men were aware,
A city's crowded thoroughfare,

And soon the central street was this
Of a renowned metropolis.

And men two centuries and a half
Trod in the footsteps of that calf.

Each day a hundred thousand rout
Followed the zigzag calf about;

And o'er his crooked journey went
The traffic of a continent.

A hundred thousand men were led
By one calf near three centuries dead.

They followed still his crooked way
And lost one hundred years a day;

For thus such reverence is lent
To well-established precedent.

A moral lesson this might teach,
Were I ordained and called to preach.

For men are prone to go it blind
Along the calf-paths of the mind,

And work away from sun to sun
To do what other men have done.

They follow in the beaten track,
And out and in and forth and back

And still their devious course pursue,
To keep the paths that others do.

But how the wise old wood-gods laugh
Who saw the first primeval calf!

Ah, many things this tale might teach—But
I am not ordained to preach.

PHILADELPHIA

I was fortunate in the city over which William Penn, in giant effigy, keeps watch and ward, in having as guide, philosopher and friend Mr. A. Edward Newton, the Johnsonian, and the author of one of the best examples of "amateur" literature that I know — "The Amenities of Book- Collecting." Mr. Newton took me everywhere, even to the little seventeenth-century Swedish church, which architecturally may be described as the antipodes of Philadelphia's newer glory, the Curtis Building, where editors are lodged like kings and can be attained to (if at all) only through marble halls. We went to St. Peter's, where, suddenly awaking during the sermon, one would think oneself to be in a London city church, and to the Historical Museum, where I found among the Quaker records many of my own ancestors and was bewildered amid such a profusion of relics of Penn, Washington and Franklin. In the old library were more traces of Franklin, including his famous electrical appliance, again testifying to the white flame with which American hero- worship can burn; and we found the sagacious Benjamin once more at the Franklin Inn Club, where the simplicity of the eighteenth century mingles with the humour and culture of the twentieth. We then drove through several miles of Fairmount Park, stopping for a few minutes in the hope of finding the late J. G. Johnson's Vermeer in the gallery there; but for the moment it was in hiding, the walls being devoted to his Italian pictures.

Finally we drew up at the gates of that strange and imposing Corinthian temple which might have been dislodged from its original site and hurled to Philadelphia by the first Quaker, Poseidon — the Girard College. This solemn fane we were permitted to enter only on convincing the porter that we were not ministers of religion — an easy enough task for Mr. Newton, who wears with grace the natural abandon of a Voltairean, but a difficult one for me. Why Stephen Girard, the worthy "merchant and mariner" who endowed this institution, was so suspicious of the cloth, no matter what its cut, I do not know; no doubt he had his reasons; but his prejudices are faithfully respected by his janitor, whose eye is a very gimlet of suspicion. However, we got in and saw the philanthropist's tomb and his household effects behind those massive columns.

That evening I spent in Mr. Newton's library among Blake and Lamb and Johnson autographs and MSS., breaking the Tenth Commandment with a recklessness that would have satisfied and delighted Stephen Girard's gatekeeper; and the next day we were off to Valley Forge to see with what imaginative thoughtfulness the Government has been transforming Washington's camp into a national park and restoring the old landmarks. It was a fine spring day and the woods were flecked with the white and pink blossoms of the dogwood—a tree which in England is only an inconspicuous hedgerow bush but here has both charm and importance and some of the unexpectedness of a tropical growth. I wish we could acclimatise it.

The memorial chapel now in course of completion on one of the Valley Forge eminences seemed to me a very admirable example not only of modern Gothic but of votive piety. And such a wealth of American symbolism cannot exist elsewhere. But in the severe little cottage where Washington made his headquarters, down by the stream, with all his frugal campaigning furniture and accessories in their old places, I felt more emotion than in the odour of sanctity. The simple reality of it conquered the stained glass.

GENERAL REFLECTIONS

Looking back on it all I realise that America never struck me as a new country, although its inhabitants often seemed to be a new people. The cities are more mature than the citizens. New York, Chicago, Boston, Philadelphia, Washington—all have an air of permanence and age. The buildings, even the most fantastic, suggest indigenousness, or at least stability; nor would the presence of more ancient structures increase this effect. To the eye of the ordinary Englishman accustomed to work in what we call the City, in Fleet Street, in the Strand, in Piccadilly, or in Oxford Street, New York would not appear to be a younger place than London, and Boston might easily strike him as older. Nor is London more than a little older, except in spots, such as the Tower and the Temple and the Abbey, and that little Tudor row in Holborn, all separated by vast tracts of modernity. Indeed, I would almost go farther and say that London sets up an illusion of being newer even than New York by reason of its more disturbing street traffic both in the roads and on the footways, and the prevalence of the gaily coloured omnibuses which thunder along so many thoroughfares in notable contrast with the sedate and sober vehicles that serve Fifth Avenue and are hardly seen elsewhere.

Meanwhile an illusion of antiquity is set up by New York's habit of commingling business houses and private residences, which surely belongs to an older order of society. In London we have done away with such a blend. Our nearest approach to Fifth Avenue is, I suppose, Regent Street; but there are no mansions among the shops of Regent Street. Our shops are there and our mansions are elsewhere, far away, in what we call residential quarters—such as Park Lane, Queen's Gate, Mayfair, the Bayswater Road, and Grosvenor Square. To turn out of Fifth Avenue into the quiet streets where people live is to receive a distinct impression of sedateness such as New York is never supposed to convey. One has the same feeling in the other great American cities.

But when it comes to their inhabitants there are to the English eye fewer signs of maturity. I have never been able to get rid of the idea that every one I have met in America, no matter how grave a senior, instead of being really and self-consciously in the thick of life, is only getting ready to begin. Perhaps this is due in part to the pleasure—the excitement almost—which American business men—and all Americans are business men—take in their work. They not merely do it, but they enjoy doing it and they watch themselves doing it. They seem to have a knack of withdrawing aside and observing themselves as from the stalls, not without applause. In other words, they dramatise continually. Now, one does not do this when one is old—it is a childish game—and it is another proof that they are younger than we, who do not enjoy our work, and indeed, most of us, are ashamed of it and want the world to believe that we live like the lilies on private means.

Similarly, many Americans seem, when they talk, to be two persons: one the talker, and the other the listener charmed by the quality of his discourse. There is nothing detrimental in such duplicity. Indeed, I think I have a very real envy of it. But one of the defects of the listening habit is perhaps to make them too rhetorical, too verbose. It is odd that the nation that has given us so much epigrammatic slang and the telegraph and the telephone and the typewriter should have so little of what might be called intellectual short-hand. But so it is. Too many Americans are remorseless when they are making themselves clear.

Yet the passion for printed idiomatic sententiousness and arresting trade-notices is visible all the time. You see it in the newspapers and in the shops. I found a children's millinery shop in New York with this laconic indication of its scope, in permanent letters, on the plate- glass window: "Lids for Kids." A New York undertaker, I am told, has affixed to all his hearses the too legible legend: "You may linger, but I'll get you yet."

When it comes to descriptive new words, coined rapidly to meet occasions, we English are nowhere compared with the Americans. Could there be anything better than the term "Nearbeer" to reveal at a blow the character of a substitute for ale? I take off my hat, too, to "crape-hanger," which leaves "kill-joy" far in the rear. But "optience" for a cinema audience, which sees but does not hear, though ingenious, is less admirable.

Although I found the walls of business offices in New York and elsewhere decorated with pithy counsel to callers, and discouragements to irrelevance, such as "Come to the point but don't camp on it," "To hell with yesterday," and so forth, I am very doubtful if with all these suggestions of practical address and Napoleonic efficiency the American business man is as quick and decisive as ours can be. There is more autobiography talked in American offices than in English; more getting ready to begin.

I have, however, no envy of the American man's inability to loaf and invite his soul, as his great democratic poet was able to do. I think that this unfamiliarity with armchair life is a misfortune. That article of furniture, we must suppose, is for older civilisations, where men have either, after earning the right to recline, taken their ease gracefully, or have inherited their fortune and are partial to idleness. It consorts ill with those who are still either continually and restlessly in pursuit of the dollar or are engaged in the occupation of watching dollars automatically arrive.

One of the things, I take it, for Americans to learn is how to transform money into a friend. So many men who ought to be quietly rejoicing in their riches seem still to be anxious and acquisitive; so many men who have become suddenly wealthy seem to be allowing their gains to ruin their happiness. For the nation's good nearly every one, I fancy, has too much money.

My experience is that England has almost everything to learn from America in the matter of hotels. I consider American second and third- class hotels to be better in many ways than our best. Every American restaurant, of each grade, is better than the English equivalent; the appointments are better, the food is served with more distinction and often is better too. When it comes to coffee, there is no comparison whatever: American coffee is the best in the world. Only quite recently has the importance of the complete suite entered the intelligence of the promoters of English hotels, and in myriads of these establishments, called first class, there is still but one bathroom to twenty rooms. Heating coils and hot and cold water in the rooms are even more rare: so rare as to be mentioned in the advertisements. Telephones in the rooms are rarer. In too many hotels in England there is still no light at the head of the bed. But we have certain advantages. For example, in English restaurants there is always something on the table to eat at once— *hors d'oeuvres* or bread and butter. In America there is too often nothing ready but iced water—an ungenial overture to any feast—and you must wait until your order has been taken. Other travellers, even Americans, have agreed with me that it would be more comfortable if the convention which decrees that the waiter shall bring everything together could be overruled. Something "to go on with" is a great ameliorative, especially when one is hungry and tired.

In thus commending American hotels over English it is, however, only right to admit that the American hotels are very much more expensive.

While on the subject of eating, I would say that for all their notorious freedoms Americans have a better sense of order than we. Their policemen may carry their batons drawn, and even swing them with a certain insolent defiance or even provocation, but New York goes on its way with more precision and less disturbance than London, and every one is smarter, more alert. The suggestion of a living wage for all is constant. It is indeed on this sense of orderliness that the success of certain of the American time-saving appliances is built. The Automat restaurants, for example, where the customer gets all his requirements himself, would never do in London. The idea is perfect; but it requires the co-operation of the customer, and that is what we should fail to provide. The spotless cleanliness and mechanical exactitude of these places in New York would cease in London, and gradually they would decline and then disappear. At heart, we in England dislike well-managed places. Nor can I see New York's public distribution of hot water adopted in London. Such little geysers as expel steam at intervals through the roadway of Fifth Avenue will never, I fear, be found in Regent Street or Piccadilly. Our communism is very patchy.

There are some unexpected differences between America and England. It is odd, for instance, to find a nation from whom we get most of our tobacco and who have the reputation of even chewing cigars, with such strict rules against smoking. In the Music Halls, which are, as a rule, better than ours, smoking is permitted only in certain parts. Public decorum again is, I should say, more noticeable in an American than an English city, and yet both in San Francisco and New York I dined in restaurants —not late—between 7 and 8— and not furtive hole-in-corner places,— where girls belonging to the establishment, wearing almost nothing at all, performed the latest dances, with extravagant and daring variations of them, among the tables. In London this kind of thing is unknown. In Paris it occurs only in the night cafés. It struck me as astonishing— and probably not at all to the good—that it should be an ordinary dinner accompaniment.

I was asked while I was in America to set down some of the chief things that I missed. I might easily have begun with walking-sticks, for until I reached New York I seemed to be the only man in America who carried one, although a San Francisco friend confessed to sometimes "wearing a cane" on Sundays. I missed a Visitors' Book either at the British Embassy in Washington or at the White House. After passing through India, where one's first duty is to enter one's name in these volumes, it seemed odd that the same machinery of civility should be lacking. I missed any system of cleaning boots during the night, in the hotels; but I soon became accustomed to this, and rather enjoyed visiting the "shine parlours," in one of which was this crisp notice: "If you like our work, tell your friends; if you don't like it, tell us." I missed gum-chewing.

But it was on returning to England that I began really to take notice. Then I found myself missing America's cleanliness, America's despatch, its hotel efficiency, its lashings of cream, its ice on every hand. All this at Liverpool! I missed later the petrol fountains all about the roads, a few of which I had seen in India, at which the motorist can replenish; but these surely will not be long in coming. I don't want England to be Americanised; I don't want America to cease to be a foreign country; but there are lessons each of us can learn.

If I were an American, although I travelled abroad now and then (and I hold that it is the duty of a man to see other lands but live in his own) I should concentrate on America. It is the country of the future. I am glad I have seen it and now know something—however slight—about it at first hand. I made many friends there and amassed innumerable delightful memories. But what is the use of eight weeks? I am ashamed not to have gone there sooner, and humiliated by the brevity of my stay. I have had the opportunity only to lift a thousand curtains, get a glimpse of the entertainment on the other side and drop them again. I should like to go there every other year and have time: time to make the acquaintance of a naturalist and learn from him the names of birds and trees and flowers; time to loiter in the byways; time to penetrate into deeper strata where intimacies strike root and the real discoveries are made; time to discern beneath the surface, so hard and assured, something fey, something wistful, the sense of tears.

INDEX

"Eha," his three books
Elephanta, caves of

Fakirs in India
Fatehpur-Sikri
Faneuil Hall, Boston
Fifth Avenue
Foss, Mr. Samuel W., his Boston poem
Franklin, Benjamin
Fujiyama
Funerals in India and England

Ganges, the
Geisha dances
Gilbert, Mr. Cass
Girard, Stephen
Goschen, Lord, wounds the tiger

Hakone, Lake
Hawking
Herford, Mr. Oliver
Hindus, the, and animals
Hokusai
Holmes, Oliver Wendell
Hong-Kong, funeral at
Honolulu
Hooghli, the
Hotels in America
Humayun's Tomb
Huntington, Mr. H. E.

Jahan, Shah, his buildings
Jains, the, their preservation of life
Japan—its lack of idlers
  and animal life
  its women
  its American reading

Otome Pass

Painters, American, in England
Parsees, the
Peacock Throne, the
Philadelphia
Pictures in America
Prince of Wales in New York
Prohibition
Pronunciation in America

Ranjitsinhji, Prince
Rickshaws
Roosevelt, Theodore, his Memorial Road
"Rose Aylmer"
Ruth, "Babe"

San Francisco
Saranac
Saturday Evening Post, the
Scott, Mr. A. P., his house
Sculpture in America
Shaw, Mr. Bernard
Simplified spelling
Skyscrapers
Skysigns
Slang in America
Snake-poison antidotes
St. Gaudens, Augustus
Stevenson, Robert Louis
Swamp-deer hunting
Swan, Mr. Thomas, his despair at Honolulu

Taj Mahal, the
Talmadge, Constance
  Norma
Tavernier on the Moguls
Theatre, the, in Japan